don't just live...

REALLY LIVE

don't just live...

REALLY LIVE

MARTIN WILES

Ambassador International
GREENVILLE, SOUTH CAROLINA & BELFAST, NORTHERN IRELAND
www.ambassador-international.com

Don't Just Live . . . Really Live

ISBN: 978-1-64960-044-8
eISBN: 978-1-64960-045-5

Cover Design by Hannah Linder Designs
Interior typesetting by Dentelle Design

AMBASSADOR INTERNATIONAL
Emerald House
411 University Ridge, Suite B14
Greenville, SC 29601, USA
www.ambassador-international.com

AMBASSADOR BOOKS
The Mount
2 Woodstock Link
Belfast, BT6 8DD, Northern Ireland, UK
www.ambassadormedia.co.uk

The colophon is a trademark of Ambassador, a Christian publishing company.

CONTENTS

INTRODUCTION

A LIST OF DOS AND don'ts. For many, this is what life entails. Don't lie. Don't cheat. Don't steal. Don't lust after what others have or people of the opposite sex. Don't swear. Or drink. Or smoke. Don't, don't, don't.

As a young elementary-age boy, I saw those rules hung neatly inside a picture frame on my bedroom wall. Don't sass Mom or Dad. Don't curse. Don't lie. I can't remember all the don'ts typed on that piece of paper, but each one had consequences. A spanking or stint in my room. Something given or something taken away. But all with the intent that I not repeat the don't. Occasionally it worked. Often, it didn't.

The plethora of don'ts colored my picture of God, since, in my case, the don'ts supposedly represented God's no-nos. The rules painted a picture of a negative and punitive Being. In my young mind, God was even stricter than my parents. Not only did Mom and Dad have their rules, but God did also—and more of them. Mom and Dad's hung in an 8x10 picture frame. God's took sixty-six books to record. I had my doubts I would ever please my parents or God sufficiently.

Many years later, I began to comprehend my connection with God wasn't about obeying the rules—although doing so was important. The connection entailed a relationship. He was a loving God, not one just waiting for me to make a slip up so He could whip me into submission. Yes, breaking His rules had consequences, but He was more interested in showing me how to really live—not just live. He wanted me to live abundantly. He was more than a God Who sat in heaven, waiting for me to mess up.

7

In reading the four gospels, I discovered I wasn't the only one with misconceptions about God. Most religious folks of Jesus' day had them, too. God was legalistic and gave nitpicky laws to obey. He wanted obedience. Period. And He needed a little assistance explaining His expectations. So the religious authorities helped Him out by adding laws and explanations—their opinions. Jesus reminded them, too, it was about the relationship, not merely rote obedience.

Two popular encounters with prominent people illustrate this misunderstanding. Nicodemus, a religious ruler, came to Jesus for a late-night talk. Without blinking an eye, Jesus told him, *I tell you the truth, unless you are born again, you cannot see the Kingdom of God* (John 3:3). Another religious leader wanted to know what he must do to gain eternal life. After Jesus listed a few of the commands, the young man proudly asserted obedience to them all. Jesus responded by instructing him to sell all he had, give it to the poor, and then follow him. The young man went away sad because he was rich (Luke 18:18–23). He obeyed the laws but missed the relationship.

Perhaps more than anywhere else in Scripture, real living is addressed and described in Jesus' Sermon on the Mount (Matthew 5–7). The teachings are demanding—and take a lifetime to master—but the rewards are bountiful. When mastered—even to a degree—life is simpler and more peaceful. Most of all, we experience the joy of knowing how to really live life. We're not artificial but genuine. And we comprehend it's not all about rules and regulations, but about a loving relationship with a loving heavenly Father through a magnificent Savior.

CHAPTER ONE

BE HAPPY . . . THE INITIAL JOURNEY

MATTHEW 5:1−6

SINCE THE BEGINNING OF TIME people have searched for the real meaning of life—happiness. Eve wasn't satisfied with the abundance of the Garden of Eden and thought she needed the forbidden fruit to complete her happiness. Some try money. Others pursue it through notoriety, power, pleasure, or immoral activities.

Experiencing the real meaning of life comes by giving up our efforts to find it and simply receiving it as God's gift. Happiness arrives through the forgiveness of our sins, which Christ paid for on Calvary. It also comes by studying and applying the practical ways He teaches to find happiness.

As Jesus begins the Sermon on the Mount, He gives a series of conditional sayings called Beatitudes which are designed to lead us to happiness. *Beatitude* isn't found in the English Bible but comes from a Latin word used by Jerome in his Latin translation.

Sadness doesn't equate with godliness and shouldn't be our constant state. Adverse circumstances may cause us to dwell temporarily "under the circumstances," but God gives us power to live above them. Nor does happiness result from changing our circumstances, but rather from trusting God to control and change them as He deems appropriate. The happiness that results from obeying the Beatitudes is not only outward, but also inward. From them we learn to be content, regardless of our circumstances.

Blessed means happy, fortunate, or blissful. The only way to experience true happiness is by possessing God's nature. Although created in God's image, His image in us is marred because of our rebellion. The only way to achieve happiness is by restoring the relationship to what it was originally. Ignoring God will never lead us to the happiness Jesus describes. Both a relationship with God and obedience to Him are necessary for happiness. While some of Jesus' sayings appear as if they might lead to misery, the result is actually the opposite.

BE POOR IN SPIRIT

Those who inherit God's kingdom are poor in spirit, but not necessarily in material possessions. One translation renders it as must *realize their need for him*. As it relates to material things, poor means reduced to begging or asking for alms. It's a picture of someone who doesn't know where their next meal or night's sleep will come from. In Jesus' day, beggars covered their faces so no one would know who they were. Poor doesn't describe a person who has little, but rather someone with nothing.

Matthew's account further explains Luke's by adding the phrase *in spirit*. This aids in understanding that there is no inherent merit in material poverty. Nor does God love the poor more than He does the wealthy. If Jesus were speaking of literal poverty, it would be un-Christlike for followers of Jesus to attempt to alleviate the burdens of the poor, starving, and destitute. By doing these things, we would abolish what brings them closer to God.

Neither does Jesus refer to having a poor-spirited attitude. Poor-spirited people lack drive and enthusiasm and have an unhealthy dose of self-esteem. Humans have value because God created us in His image. Though marred by sin, God continually works in our lives to restore the image to its proper standing. The psalmist recognized the worth of an individual when he wrote,

Thank you for making me so wonderfully complex! Your workmanship is marvelous—how well I know it (139:14).

Jesus references spiritual poverty. Our spiritual poverty must be genuine, not an act we put on in front of others. Poverty of spirit means adopting humility by letting God do surgery on our prideful areas.

We cannot enter God's Kingdom by self-effort. Only by grace do we have any hope at all. God's grace is abundant and freely offered—we have no hope of security or salvation apart from it—but it's not found in self-efficient philosophies. We must declare bankruptcy, realize our inability to meet our spiritual responsibilities, and seek help.

While a paradox, the Sermon on the Mount is for those who know they can't live up to Jesus' standards. The same was true with the law God gave in the Old Testament. No one could live by it in their own strength. God's law was designed to frustrate the individual trying so they would give up and seek God's help. The law was given to show people their sinfulness in comparison with God's requirements.

This inability to meet God's expectations was illustrated in the giving of the law on Mt. Sinai. While God delivered His commands to Moses, the people were in the valley doing the very things God forbade. Not knowing what became of Moses, the Israelites approached his brother Aaron, requesting he make them gods to follow. Aaron took their gold earrings, melted them, and constructed a golden calf. As Moses descended the mountain, he heard the celebration of pagan revelry (Exodus 32:1–8).

Great numbers of people realized their shortcomings and availed themselves of God's sacrificial system. Others refused to submit to God's standards and tried pleasing Him by their efforts. They attempted to whittle down the principles of God's law to meet their level of performance and, in the process, lowered His standards. These attempts missed the whole intent of God's law. Jesus faced this same type of hypocrisy from the religious leaders during His ministry. He was confronted time and again by those who claimed to obey the law but missed its spirit.

The story of the Pharisee and tax collector praying in the Temple illustrates this Beatitude's point well (Luke 18:9–14). All eyes focused on the Pharisee as he strutted in and made his way to the front. He thanked God he was not like other people, that he was not a sinner, and most of all, that he was not like the tax collector standing in the back. He boasted about his fasting, giving, and other acts of goodness. He was a proud man.

The tax collector, on the other hand, stood at the back and would not lift his eyes to heaven. He beat on his chest and cried out for God's mercy. He realized he could never enter God's kingdom on his own, but only by the grace of God.

Happiness involves emptying ourselves of all efforts to find happiness any other way. We must become spiritually poor before God will richly bless us. Jesus enjoyed the majesty and glory of heaven, where He resided with the Father from before time, but emptied Himself to die for our sins. Emptying must come before filling. Repentance must precede forgiveness. We recognize our unworthiness, and God accepts us.

Martin Luther, German leader of the Protestant Reformation, had a similar experience. He entered the monastery at an early age to earn his salvation through piety and good works, but he experienced failure. Only after emptying himself of personal attempts to earn salvation was God able to show him salvation was by grace alone.

Although poverty of spirit is necessary for entering God's kingdom, it's unnatural. The only avenue of change is through confrontation with a holy God. Looking at ourselves or others will never create poverty of spirit. Our hearts are corrupt and chained by sin and its destructive forces. Looking at others opens the possibility of finding someone who is no better or even worse than we are. Looking at others who have more detestable habits only makes us feel better, but fails to produce poverty of spirit.

The only way to master poverty of spirit is by looking at God as revealed in Christ. There we find true poverty of spirit and learn to say as the prophet Isaiah did, *It's all over! I am doomed, for I am a sinful man. I have filthy lips, and I live among a people with filthy lips. Yet I have seen the King, the LORD of Heaven's Armies* (6:5).

MOURN

Mourning—although not the kind we normally think about—also produces happiness. The psalmist expressed his desire for comfort after a disappointing time when he wrote, *Oh, that I had wings like a dove; then I would fly away and rest* (55:6).

Everyone faces disappointment periodically. Parents may give comfort to children in small ways, such as putting a nightlight in a dark room. Adults also experience moments when we need comfort. We lose a loved one, a friend, our job, our family, or experience a tragedy.

Sometimes, we want to call time-out, but we can't. Life continues during disappointments, trials, and failures. Since we can't take breaks, we must discover ways to find happiness in the middle of our circumstances. God divvies out the greatest comfort, and mourning invites it.

Additionally, happiness is linked with sadness. Everything we've been taught contradicts this. Jesus Himself warns against worrying (Matthew 6:25), and Paul tells us not to be anxious (Philippians 4:6). The parallel passage in Luke states, *God blesses you who weep now, for in due time you will laugh* (Luke 6:21).

Just as Jesus wasn't speaking literally but spiritually when He said the poor were happy, so He introduces a spiritual concept here also. Jesus' conception of mourning can best be described by defining what it isn't. It doesn't entail improper mourning or feeling sorry for those whose evil plans have failed or who have misguided loyalties and affections.

Amnon, one of King David's sons, offers a good example of improper mourning. His half-brother, Absalom, had a beautiful sister named Tamar, whom he fell in love with. The love Amnon had for her transformed itself into lust and passion and eventually made him sick. The Bible says, *Amnon became so obsessed with Tamar that he became ill. She was a virgin, and Amnon thought he could never have her* (2 Samuel 13:2). His improper mourning led to rape.

Improper mourning can occur when losing a loved one. Mourning when loved ones die is a natural and necessary process, but when taken to an extreme, can be very devastating. We can mourn to the extent we become incapacitated. Instead of learning to adapt to our new circumstances, we mourn for extended periods of time, eventually coming to the place where we can't function in society. This then becomes a selfish endeavor.

To mourn when facing death or disappointment can be proper or improper, and we determine which. A life wherein happiness was constant would really be unhappy, for disappointments are the spices of life. Pain prods us on and leads to investigation. Through sorrow, we learn to appreciate the good things in life. By disappointments, our sensitivity to the disappointments of others is increased. Disappointments can even drive us to Christ.

But the above definitions probably fall short of what Jesus had in mind. Our mourning must include others. We should have a social conscience, which involves mourning over the world's evil. Christian means to be Christ-like and to be Christ-like involves caring for others by mourning over their evil and sorrow. Our walk with Christ should produce in us sound social consciences. Christ cared for others and we must also. Jesus said, *Love your enemies! Pray for those who persecute you* (Matthew 5:44).

Christ-followers should never stand aloof or criticize social movements which honestly endeavor to help those with needs they can't meet. While the need for salvation is primary, people have many secondary needs that become primary before they can or will properly listen to the gospel.

But mourning for others isn't merely concern for their salvation. Proper mourning involves concern over inequalities: racial, social, or otherwise. We mourn for those who destroy natural resources and violate ethical standards

·in politics, medicine, business, and religion. Mourning entails involvement in our world.

While mourning for others is a part of Jesus' meaning, mourning over sin is probably the primary meaning. We need godly sorrow. The Greek word for mourn is reserved for the most severe and strongest type of mourning—the kind experienced when losing a loved one.

Intense mourning is characteristic of those who belong to God's family and those who wish to. Mourning applies to nonbelievers—who recognize their sin and need of repentance and in sorrow turn to God—and also to believers—who mourn when they sin against God and express sorrow. Spiritual mourning enables us to see our unworthiness before God. This naturally flows from practicing the first Beatitude of poverty in spirit.

This type of mourning was at the center of Jesus' message. As He entered the synagogue at Nazareth and began His formal ministry, He read from the scroll of Isaiah which said, *The Spirit of the LORD is upon me, for he has anointed me to bring Good News to the poor. He has sent me to proclaim that captives will be released, that the blind will see, that the oppressed will be set free* (Luke 4:18). The captivity was enslavement to sin, and He came to deliver people from its grip.

The gospels record Jesus weeping over sin at least twice: first, when death took His good friend Lazarus (John 11), and, second, when He witnessed the sin and hardness of heart of those in Jerusalem (Luke 19:41). Mourning, as Jesus did, is a wonderful practice that leads to happiness.

For the unbeliever who mourns over their sin, repents of it, and trusts Christ as their Savior, comfort comes in knowing Christ accepts them and grants forgiveness. For believers, we have the comfort of knowing all our sins have been forgiven at the cross. They have no power over us anymore. Although we will not live a sinless life, we do not live a life of defeat either. We can triumph over sin as we live the abundant life Jesus promises, experiencing the power of His resurrection through our lives.

The final comfort involves realizing one day that all sin, and its effects, will be obliterated from our lives and the world. Pride, suffering, hate, sickness, and death will end. We will leave the world as we know it and enter Christ's presence.

BE GENTLE

Happy people—those who know about real living—are also gentle. This trait is often misunderstood and wrongly interpreted. Aristotle, a Greek thinker and philosopher of the fourth century B. C., defined the virtues of life as being somewhere in the middle between an excess display of a virtue and a complete lack of that same virtue. For him, gentleness was somewhere between excessive anger on the one hand and an absence of any anger at all on the other hand.

This trait takes us a step farther in the effort to live as God designs and must be added to poverty of spirit and mourning. Jesus' instruction is foreign to our usual way of thinking and acting. He says happiness is connected to a gentle spirit. Pride and revenge are the normal responses to conflict, not gentleness or turning the other cheek. We look out for personal interests, not the interests of others. Additionally, we do not normally allow others to treat us unfairly without justice or revenge.

Jesus' peers weren't any different. They were proud and looked for a conquering Messiah to deliver them from their enemies and restore what they assumed was their rightful place in the world. The Messiah would deal with the Romans who oppressed them.

All religious sects of Jesus' day looked for the Messiah, but each had different expectations. Pharisees looked for the Messiah to dramatically appear and deliver the Jews from bondage to Rome. Sadducees anticipated a Messiah who would arrange a political compromise with the Romans. Essenes withdrew from society into their own little groups. Zealots violently opposed Roman bondage and craved a military Messiah.

They didn't expect, nor desire, a Messiah with a gentle spirit. Since they weren't looking for a humble Messiah, they didn't accept or understand Jesus. They didn't identify the Messiah with the Suffering Servant Isaiah spoke of. Nor were they looking for a Messiah who allowed His rights to be violated and who would die on a cross. When advocating gentleness, Jesus was only asking us to follow His example.

Gentleness is not a natural characteristic of humanity in our sinful condition, but rather a supernatural working of God's Spirit. The word means mild or soft and involves the idea of soothing medicine or a gentle blowing breeze. Some manufacturers apply the word to their paper products. When applied to individuals, gentle means submissive, quiet, and tenderhearted.

Jesus displayed this spirit when making His triumphal entry into Jerusalem by riding a donkey instead of a white horse. He was not a military leader coming to conquer, nor was He coming to stand up for His rights but to lay down His life.

At the same time, gentleness doesn't mean cowardly, weak, or spiritless. Jesus wasn't any of these. Gentleness means having high spirits, courage, and great strength. While it is never acceptable to be angry when we suffer personal insult or injury, it is always right to be angry when others do.

Gentleness also involves behavior. The word was used to describe domesticated animals who accepted their master's control and were properly behaved, such as circus animals. Gentleness was also used to describe people belonging to society's upper crust because they were usually polite, balanced, and well mannered—the same traits that should characterize us.

A final idea involves a subservient and trusting attitude toward God. This is probably the primary meaning and reminds us we are sinners unworthy of God's grace and mercy. Realizing this, we turn our eyes to God and see His holiness and righteousness. We have a proper vertical view and therefore acquire a right horizontal outlook.

Jesus proclaimed a kingdom characterized by gentleness. Though many did not accept this style of living, it has been God's way from the beginning. Eliphaz, while speaking to Job, said of God, *He gives prosperity to the poor and protects those who suffer* (Job 5:11). Moses was humble, and his humility pleased God (Numbers 12:3). The psalmist wrote, *He leads the humble in doing right, teaching them his way* (Psalm 25:9).

Gentleness is power under control. The gentle are free of violence and vengeance and have died to selfish desires. They are interested in looking out for others more than for themselves. Serving others brings them joy. Even when insulted or injured, they love rather than retaliate. Though the gentle person has power to insult and abuse for wrongs committed, they control that power by surrendering it to God.

Meekness (gentleness) is not a trait we can take or leave and expect to live this real life. Gentleness is necessary for salvation. Until we humble ourselves before God and admit our helplessness, we cannot be saved.

Meekness is necessary for sharing God's love because pride always stands in the way. And meekness is necessary for our lives to bring God glory. When proud, we edify ourselves, not him.

The reward for gentleness is inheriting the earth. This doesn't mean we will own oil wells, live the lifestyle of the rich and famous, or own blocks of downtown Manhattan, New York. In a sense, we do inherit the earth now because, as God's children, we actually own all things, though we don't currently possess them. The meek individual is content with what God provides. God owns the world's treasures, and Christians are joint heirs with Christ. With this in mind, we need to care for all God entrusts to us.

Jesus' primary reference entails the future. Paul says saints will judge the world (1 Corinthians 6:2). We endure sorrow and suffering now, but when Christ returns, we will rule and reign with Him while enjoying a new heaven and earth.

God originally gave people the responsibility of dominion over His creation, but this was quickly distorted through rebellion and disobedience.

In the future world, we will once again be able to do that which God initially commanded.

HUNGER AND THIRST FOR THE RIGHT THINGS

Ironically, happiness is also connected to hunger and thirst. For untold years, hunger and starvation have been chronic problems for people in various countries. Even with our technological advances, hunger still stalks. Many regularly go to bed hungry, and the homeless wander the streets of every city, large and small. Yet physical hunger and thirst pale in comparison to a more serious hunger and thirst everyone possesses, whether recognized or not.

Building on the prior negatives, Jesus now strikes a positive note. When putting aside our selfish endeavors, sins, and self-centered power pursuits, we naturally hunger and thirst for Christ's righteousness. Hungering and thirsting for the things of God leads to real living. The hunger and thirst Jesus references is intense, such as the kind those in famine lands endure. Not only should the hunger and thirst be intense, but also a continual longing for our lives be holy like Christ's.

Sadly, things can interfere with and weaken our desire for righteousness. We get entangled in worldly pursuits and realize hungering and thirsting for Jesus' righteousness would mean changing plans, priorities, and lifestyles. Tragically, many turn to other things for satisfaction, such as alcohol, drugs, immorality, pornography, crime, and a host of other perversions.

Moses talked with God face to face. He observed the miraculous things God performed in Egypt and on the way to the Promised Land. Even though he experienced all this, he still desired more knowledge of God's righteousness. Paul was a man whose life God worked in marvelously. In spite of witnessing the resurrected Christ, traveling on several missionary journeys, and being commissioned to carry the gospel to the Gentile world, he still desired to be clothed with more of Christ's righteousness.

The key to spiritual thirst is never to be satisfied. Our passion should always be a closer walk with God, and this is possible because there's always room for improvement. The righteousness we hunger for is vital to our spiritual life, just as food and water are to physical existence.

Unbelievers may not always appear as if they are starving for spiritual things, but this is because the wicked enjoy the side effects of living in a world created by God and inhabited by His people. They get some fringe benefits because of believers. Possessions, good health, freedom of religion, opportunities for advancement and success, knowledge, and other benefits are theirs because of God's common grace. Some of the greatest minds of history have rejected God. Many take God's blessings and use them selfishly.

God admonishes believers not to love the world or the things of it. We must hunger for spiritual things and use His blessings to honor and give Him glory. The Bible says, *For the world offers only a craving for physical pleasure, a craving for everything we see, and pride in our achievements and possessions. These are not from the Father, but are from this world* (1 John 2:16).

So necessary is this hunger that it proves our identity. When we strive to be what God wants and have a driving passion to obey him, we can rest assured we belong to God. This hunger is a necessity, not an option. Along with it is the understanding that we don't have the power to live the Christian life alone but must allow God to live it through us.

The first goal of spiritual hunger and thirst is salvation. When we sincerely realize our position and destiny apart from God, we turn to Him for salvation. The result is happiness as we discover forgiveness from our sins.

The second goal is sanctification. This is a lifelong process where we grow in our spiritual walk and, at the same time, realize we never achieve perfection until we're home in heaven. Being declared righteous by God because of our faith in Christ does not mean we are always righteous in our actions and attitudes.

When we hunger and thirst for Christ's righteousness, we receive it in full and are satisfied. Although satisfied, we must continue to hunger and thirst for more of Christ's righteousness—somewhat like eating steak or other foods we enjoy. After eating a juicy piece of steak, we are satisfied momentarily, but this does not mean we will never desire steak again.

CHAPTER TWO

BE HAPPY . . . THE CONTINUING JOURNEY

MATTHEW 5:7–12

THE FIRST FOUR BEATITUDES DEAL with inner principles that, if followed, will result in outward actions, which should be our goal. Realizing our spiritual poverty apart from Christ naturally leads to showing mercy. Those who recognize the horribleness of sin strive for purity. Not seeking retaliation or revenge results in peace. And striving to live by God's standards will incur persecution.

SHOW MERCY

Having others show us mercy is wonderful and refreshing, but it's also important to show them mercy in return. This is the way life should operate. In order to enjoy real living, we must reciprocate God's mercy.

When Jesus says to be merciful, He refers to beneficial acts toward others. Compassion is also involved. We help the helpless and care for those afflicted with the pains and problems of this world. Jesus gives the greatest example of what He teaches by going to the cross. Beyond that, He shows it by giving us daily mercy.

In demonstrating mercy, our motives and intentions are important. We should not perform merciful acts because we have guilty consciences or ulterior motives. When reaching out to help the less fortunate, we do so from a heart of love, not guilt over having more than they do.

Neither should mercy be designed to impress. Announcing to the world what we've done destroys the purity of the act. Our motive is not garnering praise, a pat on the back, a pin, or a plaque. If these are our motives, praise from others will be our only reward. We perform merciful acts because we love God and others.

Jesus faced merciless acts and complete misunderstanding from many. The typical teaching in His time was to love only those who loved in return. But Jesus taught this attitude would not lead to life as He intends.

When we show mercy only to get something in return, we miss the word's meaning, as well as the reward. We show mercy expecting nothing in return because we love others as God does. Expecting a return demonstrates our selfishness. Everyone reciprocating our care would be wonderful. Unfortunately, God's Word and experience teach differently. Nowhere do we find the promise that others will be merciful to us if we are to them. We may seldom or never receive a thank you for a kind deed or payment for services rendered.

Jesus did not always get kind responses either. He healed the blind, lame, deaf, and sick. He allowed prostitutes, tax collectors, drunkards, and the worst kind of sinners to experience His forgiveness. In return, He was misunderstood, gossiped about, and ultimately crucified.

Mercy doesn't always come from others, but it is guaranteed from God. Showing mercy with correct motives invites God's mercy into our life. Not only do we receive blessings from him, but we will also discover true happiness by helping others. Special feelings result when doing something good from the heart.

The Romans didn't think highly of this attribute. They classified mercy as a disease of the soul and a sign of weakness. When Roman children were born, fathers decided whether or not they lived. The Romans also had this option for slaves. For good reasons or no reason, they could order a slave put to death without threat of arrest or reprisal. The same held true for their wives. If a Roman wife provoked her husband, he could order her executed.

But real living continually shows mercy—even to people who may be unloving in return. Showing mercy results in happiness and more mercy from God, and the ways we show it are as multifaceted as people because we respond differently to various situations.

We demonstrate mercy through physical acts. The story of the Good Samaritan is a wonderful example (Luke 10:25–37). Thieves beat, robbed, and left a man for dead. A priest passed by but neglected his chance to show mercy. Likewise a Levite wandered by but also overlooked the opportunity. Finally, a half-breed and hated Samaritan appeared and showed mercy by bandaging the man's wounds, taking him to a nearby inn, and paying the innkeeper to care for him. He also promised to reimburse the innkeeper at a later date for any expenses above his original payment. Physical acts of mercy also include feeding the hungry, clothing the needy, and visiting the sick and those in prison.

We show mercy with an attitude that refuses to hold grudges and that resolves resentment. We should not major on other's faults and failures but on their good qualities. We are all prone to make mistakes and need to hold each other up, not tear each other down.

Mercy and unforgiveness are mutually exclusive. Mercy is shown by immediately forgiving those who we may feel justified in not forgiving because they treated us unjustly. But we do it anyway because God forgives us.

Mercy shows up in spiritual ways. We should pray for and share God's love with those who don't know Christ. Jesus prayed for those crucifying Him and saved the thief who asked Jesus to remember him. We show it by lovingly confronting others with the offer of forgiveness. We must let them know we and God desire a relationship with them. As we share God's mercy, we receive more from Him. We enjoy the happiness of seeing people come to know Christ as their Savior and also experience the joy of meeting people's needs in His name.

Shakespeare defined mercy in a well-known speech by Portia in the play, *The Merchant of Venice:*

The quality of mercy is not strained
It droppeth as the gentle rain from heaven
Upon the place beneath. It is twice blessed:
It blesses him that gives and him that takes.
'Tis mightiest in the mightiest; it becomes
The throned monarch better than his crown.

Jesus illustrated the importance of showing mercy when He told of a slave forgiven by a king (Matthew 18:21–35). The slave owed a debt he couldn't pay, but after begging for mercy, the king released him from paying it. He immediately went to a fellow slave, who owed him far less than he owed the king, and demanded payment. When the second slave begged for mercy, the forgiven slave denied it and threw him into prison. When the king heard, he rebuked the forgiven slave for not showing the same mercy he was shown.

BE PURE IN HEART

People with greenhouses normally sell flowers and shrubbery or just want to keep flowers year round. Temperatures in a greenhouse are warm and constant. This environment protects sensitive vegetation from such things as frost and the sun's harmful rays. Plants grow faster, more efficiently, and healthier in greenhouses. But suppose I gathered seeds from weeds and planted them in my greenhouse. People might question my sanity because I said I wanted a greenhouse filled with flowers and fruit.

Jesus says the pure in heart will see God. Later, He tells a parable of a farmer sowing seed (Matthew 13:1–23). Some seed fell on the footpath meandering between the fields. The dirt was packed, which prevented the seed from penetrating. Birds swooped down and devoured the seed. Other seed fell on shallow soil made so by underlying rock. Though it germinated, there was no depth for the roots, and the plants soon withered and died. Still more seed fell on ground infested with thorns. The seed sprouted but was choked by thorns. However, the seed that fell on good ground sprouted, produced plants, and bore fruit.

Jesus teaches the importance of pure hearts in both passages. Only in pure hearts can He scatter His teachings and expect fruit. Only when pure in heart can we encounter God. With impure spiritual hearts, we cannot function correctly or be used adequately by God—just as a damaged physical heart will impair activities.

Pure hearts are important in our service to God. When Jesus speaks of a pure heart, he's not referencing the literal organ or it being in perfect condition. In God's world, we can have bad physical hearts and good spiritual hearts simultaneously. Terms more familiar to us are mind, will, or emotions.

If I sow weed seeds in my greenhouse, I will reap weeds, not plants, flowers, or fruit. If we sow bad things in our hearts and minds, we will reap unhealthy results. What proceeds from our mouths or in our actions comes from the inside. When our hearts and minds are evil, wickedness comes out. We cannot consistently be on the outside what we aren't on the inside.

Our hearts and minds are magnificent gifts from God. The reason the Bible classifies them as evil is because of our sinful nature. Originally, they were pure and can be again by receiving Christ's forgiveness and feeding them godly things. Our minds are also perfectly suited for growing things just as the greenhouse is, but like the flowers or plants in a greenhouse, they must be managed.

Thoughts produce actions. Some thoughts bloom like beautiful flowers while others produce weeds. Sowing seeds of hope will result in an optimistic outlook on life while thoughts of doubt grow pessimism. An optimist sees a glass half full while a pessimist views it as half empty. Optimists hope while pessimists worry. Optimists encourage and pessimists complain.

Since our hearts and minds are like greenhouses, we must be careful what we sow. Solomon says to guard our hearts because it affects everything we do (Proverbs 4:23). This is true in the spiritual and physical realm. Several scenarios illustrate this truth. Two people stuck in a traffic jam may react differently. One might become angry because his schedule has been altered while the other sees it as an opportunity to slow down.

Man in a Hurry was an *Andy Griffith* episode illustrating this truth also. An important Charlotte businessman's car broke down just outside of Mayberry on Sunday. Since it was Sunday, mechanical work was impossible. He became stressed over his situation until Gomer's cousin Goober finally repaired his car. By this time, Mayberry's slow, relaxed pace had influenced him, and he decided to spend the night anyway.

Or imagine two mothers who face the same tragedy. One is destroyed and convinces herself she will never get over it. The other expresses faith God will sustain her. Or two executives who face success. One congratulates himself, believing his ingenuity is responsible, while the other gives God the credit.

Our minds are the dwelling place of God's Spirit, and we must guard them carefully. Thought management is essential. We hear a great deal about time management, weight management, and personnel management, but little about thought management. Anger, revenge, self-pity, and lust never grow beautiful flowers.

Jesus exemplified thought management. When the crowd attempted to make Him king, He rejected their intentions and kept out arrogance (John 6:15). On another occasion, when telling His followers about His coming demise, Peter rebuked Him. Jesus classified Peter as acting like Satan and told him to get behind Him, rejecting the thought that there was an alternate way to pay for our sins (Matthew 16:23). Paul says our attitude should parrot Jesus' (Philippians 2:5). Our thoughts should be submitted to Christ's authority.

When we think things we have done are beyond God's forgiveness, Jesus reminds us we are never beyond forgiveness. When tempted to commit ungodly actions, we remember Jesus says wrong is never right.

Paul writes, *We destroy every proud obstacle that keeps people from knowing God. We capture their rebellious thoughts and teach them to obey Christ*

(2 Corinthians 10:5). While difficult in practice, if God agrees with thoughts, we allow them. If He doesn't, we kick them out. Through Bible study, we compare the right or wrongfulness of our thoughts.

BE A PEACEMAKER

The search for peace in our personal lives and in the world is ancient. Beauty contest participants once gave a common answer when asked what they wanted: world peace. Acts of terror and violence, remind us that instability in our world is abundant.

Research has shown that from thirty-six years prior to Jesus' birth until 1968, there were 14,553 known wars. Since 1945, seventy or more wars and more than 200 outbreaks of violence have occurred. The United States of America has fought the Civil War, two World Wars, a Korean conflict, the Vietnam War, Persian Gulf War, and the ongoing war against terrorism.

As much as we desire peace, it seems to escape our grasp. Though peace is our goal, society seems to applaud violence. We live with it as a way of life. Television, theaters, and the internet promote it. Violent material garners higher ratings.

Jesus' kingdom needs peacemakers. Mastering the practice encapsulates real living. God's Word portrays peace in the beginning and at the end. The first humans enjoyed it, and the final state will exude it. In the meantime, wars and violence will reign. Sin is the reason for the absence of peace, but the solution is not escaping the world. Peace is found by confronting difficult situations and searching for peaceful solutions. As we strive for outward peace, we demonstrate the inner peace found in Christ.

The Jewish people greet one another with the word, "shalom"—a word that means the person saying it desires that the individual spoken to have all the peace and goodness God can give. When Jesus commands peacemaking, He's telling us to establish love and harmony between individuals. He desires our involvement in resolving wrong attitudes and actions. The writer of

Hebrews said, *Work at living in peace with everyone, and work at living a holy life, for those who are not holy will not see the Lord* (12:14).

Peace only results individually and with others when our lives are characterized by God's holiness. Otherwise, we stir up strife and react with vengeance and retaliation. We can only imagine what a greater measure of peace would result if all international and local leaders understood Jesus' meaning of peacemaking.

At the same time, Christ is not speaking of peace at any price. Jesus also said He came not to bring peace but division (Matthew 10:34). Good cannot be compromised with evil to bring peace. Overlooking evil to obtain peace isn't acceptable, and the means do not always justify the ends. Peace must come on God's terms, not ours.

Sin, and its many manifestations, is the great enemy of peace. The presence of sin causes turmoil and division, while the absence of sin in the final state is the reason peace will reign. As peacemakers, we can't truly offer peace without first making people aware of their need to make peace with God. This is a prerequisite of having peace personally and being able to live at peace with others.

Jesus' encounter with the Samaritan woman is a good example (John 4). The Jews hated the Samaritans because they were racially mixed. Since no love existed between them, peace proved elusive. As Jesus traveled through the region of Samaria, He tried to make peace with a local woman, but the focal point was on what basis and terms He could establish peace. Jesus confronted her first with her spiritual need. When she accepted Him as Savior, peace flooded her life. Now, she could live at peace with others.

God is the one who brings peace into our lives so that we live at peace with others. Lack of world and individual peace is really a lack of God. Jesus reconciles individuals to the Father and then to others. He is the way to the Father, and without Him there is no peace. He can lead us to peaceful relationships with folks we never thought possible. He is our mediator and great High Priest. The shape of the cross illustrates the peace possible with

God and others. Here the righteousness of Christ overcame sin and made peace available.

When Jesus ascended into heaven, He sent the Spirit as an agent of peace. The Father is the source of peace, Jesus manifested peace, and the Spirit brings peace into our lives. By accepting this, we can hope to live at peace with others.

The believer's peace is unique and experienced even in turmoil. Things happening around us shouldn't affect the peace within us because God's peace transcends all understanding and comprehension. Circumstances do not bring it or prevent it.

We can be messengers of God's peace by making peace with God, by leading others to God's peace, by making peace with others, and by looking for points of agreement.

Many will reject our offer of peace through a relationship with Christ, but this doesn't mean we cannot live at peace with them. Although we cannot compromise our beliefs, we can usually reach points of agreement. Through love and patience, they may eventually come to know God's peace.

Every Christian is responsible for being a peacemaker and happiness results when we are. Life is more enjoyable when we live harmoniously rather than fight. Although complete world peace will be elusive, we can know more peace than conflict when we seek peace with God and others.

BE WILLING TO FACE PERSECUTION

When Jesus speaks about persecution, He reaches the pinnacle of the happiness ladder and demonstrates the irony of real living. We don't imagine happiness coming from persecution, but Jesus says it does. And the Bible and Christian history exemplify it.

Persecution is not optional for the Christ follower. When living godly, we experience it. A wonderful contrast is the account of the apostles leaving the Sanhedrin (Jewish High Court) after a flogging and *rejoicing that God had counted them worthy to suffer disgrace for the name of Jesus* (Acts 5:41).

Living godly confronts evil head on and thereby invites persecution. Abel and Moses are honorable biblical examples. Abel lived a godly life, and his brother Cain killed him. Moses desired identification with his people, but ended up on the backside of the desert because he killed an enemy. Following God is a costly endeavor, and it is an injustice to teach otherwise. Doing so entails great sacrifice but results in great rewards.

Persecution may be physical or verbal. We may be asked to cut our work quality on the job, or to do something that conflicts with our faith. We may be asked to lie. It could be our refusal to listen to off-color jokes or our resistance to sexual advances. Refusing these or similar things may lead to ostracism or being made fun of. The various forms of persecution are not really against us but the One we serve.

First-century Roman emperor, Nero, accused Christians of being traitors who set fire to Rome. He covered them with pitch and set them afire as torches in his garden. Believers were accused of cannibalism for observing the Lord's Supper and of having sexual orgies because they celebrated with love feast meals. Romans also accused them of being revolutionaries because they claimed Jesus as Lord instead of the emperor.

Persecution evidences our salvation. *For you have been given not only the privilege of trusting in Christ but also the privilege of suffering for him* (Philippians 1:29). Praise and acceptance from unbelievers should alert us that something is amiss.

Fortunately, persecution is not constant. Jesus was not continually opposed, and periods of popularity may come for us as well. Nor should we be obnoxious or reflect martyr complexes. However, we should not be surprised by persecution or attempt to conceal our beliefs to avoid it. Jesus said, *If anyone is ashamed of me and my message, the Son of Man will be ashamed of that person when he returns in his glory and in the glory of the Father and the holy angels* (Luke 9:26).

Enduring persecution assures we will inherit the kingdom of heaven. Our blessing is double: happiness and eternity with Christ. The blessings of comfort, strength, and joy are present, but greater blessings are in store.

Comfort in times of persecution comes by remembering that godly saints before us were treated the same and by looking forward to our great reward in heaven. Real living demands it.

CHAPTER THREE

BE AN EFFECTIVE INFLUENCE

MATTHEW 5:13–16

JOHN DONNE SAID, "NO MAN is an island."

Elihu Burrit wrote, "No human being can come into this world without increasing or diminishing the sum total of human happiness, not only of the present but of every subsequent age of humanity."

We cannot deny our influence on others and the world. We do not have a choice. Whether we are popular or unknown is irrelevant. What we can choose is whether or not our influence is positive or negative, healthy or unhealthy. When we really live, we produce a good influence. Inconsistency and complacency, on the other hand, birth a life of disappointment.

Christians have the responsibility and privilege to be real. Our actions could even color someone's response to the gospel. While we must influence unbelievers, we cannot adopt or reflect their lifestyles. John ponders this when he writes, *Do not love this world nor the things it offers you, for when you love the world, you do not have the love of the Father in you* (1 John 2:15).

We carry the message of life and should permeate the world as salt does food. Jesus' statement that we are salt and light presupposes the world needs these influences—and it does because of sin's impact. Not only is there something wrong with the world system, but there is also something wrong with people.

The world needs salt because it is corrupted with wickedness, and it needs light because it is overrun by sin's darkness—conditions that will only worsen. Paul writes, *But evil people and impostors will flourish. They will deceive others and will themselves be deceived* (2 Timothy 3:13).

Nor have advancements improved our sinful nature. In fact, technological improvements have led to more creative ways to disobey God's commands. More knowledge often brings increased wickedness.

In Noah's day wickedness was so intense that God could stand it no longer, so He sent a flood as punishment. *The LORD observed the extent of human wickedness on the earth, and he saw that everything they thought or imagined was consistently and totally evil* (Genesis 6:5). Shortly after, He destroyed Sodom and Gomorrah for their wickedness. David also recognized the presence of a sinful nature: *For I was born a sinner—yes, from the moment my mother conceived me* (Psalm 51:5).

Humanity is sinking, not evolving to a higher level of goodness. People are not only affected by sin but also contribute to the problem. While not as badly as we could be, we are still infected. Disbelieving what the Bible teaches about why the world needs salt and light provided the foundation for Communism's philosophy.

Communism is based on the assumed goodness of individuals. Creating the right circumstances allows this goodness to rise to the top. When it does, all people will work for the good of others. Everyone will have what they need, and class distinctions will disappear, as will rivalries. While the philosophy sounds good, and even looks good on paper, it doesn't work because it is based on the faulty premise that humanity is inherently good.

Jesus' command to be salt and light is a directive to dominate. The question is not whether we will be salt or light but how effective we are as those substances. We can translate the verse, *You are the only salt of the earth, and you are the only light of the world.*

Adopting the characteristics of these elements gives us tremendous responsibility. Salt can kill, enhance, and preserve. Rock salt will kill grass, but flavors boiled peanuts. Table salt enhances food's flavor and can also be used to preserve meat, but too much can result in health problems.

Christians are separated from the world by our position and lifestyle but are also connected with it. We are the only hope the world has, and, because of this, we must ensure our influence is effective. God's church and His standards must get into the world rather than the reverse. Good influences are different from what they influence.

But believers are not required to season and shine alone. We are not individual grains of salt or rays of light, nor are we lone rangers. Only as we join hands and remember our common task can our collective influence be realized.

Salt was important in the ancient world. Romans were often paid in salt. Salt was also used as a mark of friendship and in the binding of covenants. As salt relates to believers, Jesus could have meant for us to live pure lives, add attractiveness to the gospel, or sting the unsaved with the gospel message as salt does an open wound. What He probably meant was that we should act as preservatives, retarding and hindering the growth of evil. Believers should exhibit a good spiritual influence, making the world a better place because we are citizens.

Light illuminates what it shines upon. Jesus was the light of the world, and we are His reflection. As we spread the gospel message, we make our light noticeable. Jesus said, *You are the light of the world—like a city on a hilltop that cannot be hidden. No one lights a lamp and then puts it under a basket. Instead, a lamp is placed on a stand, where it gives light to everyone in the house* (Matthew 5:14–15).

Inherent in Jesus' command is the possibility of failure. Salt can lose its saltiness or become flat through contamination with other materials. While we cannot stop being salt, we can lose our effectiveness by allowing ourselves to be influenced rather than influencing.

Light can't not be light, but we can hide our light and become ineffective. This happens when we are indifferent, loveless, and careless in our lifestyles. Our purpose is glorifying and praising God and leading others to do the same.

When we season and shine effectively, we are successful in our efforts to be real Christians, and we live life as God intends.

CHAPTER FOUR

LIVE AND DIE BY THE WORD

MATTHEW 5:17–20

OPINIONS ABOUT GOD'S WORD HAVE divided believers and unbelievers for centuries. French Emperor Napoleon said, "The gospel is not a book; it is a living being, with an action, a power, which invades everything that opposes its extension, behold! It is upon this table: This book, surpassing all others. I never omit to read it, and every day with some pleasure."

Voltaire, French infidel and philosopher, is famous for claiming Christianity would be swept into nonexistence within one hundred years of his death. However, within fifty years of his demise, the Geneva Bible Society was using his house and printing press to produce Bibles.

I come from a long line of family members who were people of the Book. My great-grandmother on my father's side was a woman of the Book. For as long as I can remember, she lived with my grandparents. She had her own bedroom, just off the living room, and she reposed there often. As I sat and talked with her, I noticed the Book either lying open on her bed or closed on her night stand. She devoured it religiously. I now have that Book to which she clung dearly.

Both of my grandparents on my father's side were also people of the Book. My grandmother's Bible lay on the end table beside the couch on the end where she sat. If not there, it lay on the couch beside her, open to passages she studied for the Sunday school class she taught. I now have her Bible. My grandfather's Bible lay on the nightstand beside his bed. After retiring for the night, he turned on a solitary lamp and read from the Book. I also have his Book. Based on my personal experience with my immediate family, I can say Voltaire was mistaken. Additionally, within fifty years of Voltaire's demise, the Evangelical Society of Geneva used his house to store Bibles and gospel tracts. And, in an even greater twist of fate—or providence—the printing presses Voltaire used to spew his propaganda were used to print Bibles.

Battles over words such as infallibility and trustworthy are fought intelligently and intensely. Some propose the Bible is accurate in every matter it addresses, while others maintain its accuracy only when it speaks to spiritual issues. Others pick and choose what to interpret literally and what to view as symbolic. The question, "Does the Bible contain God's Word or is it God's Word," sums up the matter. Yet what we think is not nearly as important as what Jesus says about it here in Matthew and what is written about it in other places.

God's Word is everlasting—not individual Bibles themselves, but whom the Bible points to as the Word, Jesus. John makes this evident when he writes, *In the beginning the Word already existed. The Word was with God, and the Word was God* (John 1:1). Even if every Bible in the world was destroyed, God's Word would still exist. As long as Christ lives, God's Word survives. If every Bible were destroyed, God's Word would still inhabit a believer's heart.

Really living as a believer entails understanding the importance of God's Word and adhering to its principles. It is not about Bibliology—worshipping the Bible—but about worshipping the One the entire story points to. God's Word is preeminent above all other literature and philosophies.

Societies must have rules, they must be absolute, and truth must govern them. When we destroy the absolute nature of rules, it leads to questioning and even discarding them, resulting in sporadic and uneven application. This is called situational ethics. Each individual determines what is right and wrong, and we also accept what others believe without question.

Eliminating references to God removes the ultimate standard for truth. Truth may appear in places other than God's Word, but all truth exists only because of God's Word. Before the recording of Scripture, God's truth and His character were visible in nature. These laws, along with God's written record, place emphasis on His preeminence rather than that of humans. Humanism, on the other hand, places humanity in the limelight, making them judges of right and wrong. The result is less need for God—or no need at all.

God's standards cannot be reduced to fit ours. Rather, we must work to meet His. His Word is not outdated and is more than a compilation of people's ideas. God's Word is preeminent because He authored it. Jesus refers to the Old Testament as God's Word. In His time, this was the only Bible. A later writer applies it to the finished product: *Above all, you must realize that no prophecy in Scripture ever came from the prophet's own understanding, or from human initiative. No, those prophets were moved by the Holy Spirit, and they spoke from God* (2 Peter 1:21).

Neither Jesus' intention nor His purpose was abolishing the moral law or the Ten Commandments. The Pentateuch (first five books of the Old Testament) contains the moral and ceremonial laws of God, and the prophets expounded and affirmed both. These laws confronted people about sin, using God's Word as a basis. They also warned of God's imminent judgment if people chose not to obey.

Christ accomplished the law by reiterating it to the people, by keeping it Himself, and by clarifying the misapplications and misinterpretations attached to it by the religious leaders. Their traditions made the law a burden that God never designed it to be.

These toilsome circumstances arose out of the seventy years Israel spent in Babylonian captivity. Historians conclude that Jews essentially lost the Hebrew language during this time and adopted Aramaic, which lasted up to and beyond Jesus' time. The average Jew depended on rabbis to read and interpret the Hebrew language for them, much as worshippers depended on priests to read and interpret the Latin scriptures for them in the time prior to the Protestant Reformation. This situation allowed the rabbis to build an entire system based on the ignorance of the people. The religion of the Jews that Jesus faced in His time period was a product of the rabbi's oral tradition, which is why Jesus often uttered His "You have heard it said, but I say" teachings.

Jesus also references the permanence of the Word. God's Word will remain and outlive time. To illustrate this, Jesus uses the jot and tittle. The jot is the smallest letter of the Greek and Hebrew alphabet and about the size of the English apostrophe. The tittle is a small stroke used to distinguish one Hebrew letter from another.

While Christians are not bound by Jewish ceremonial laws, we are bound by the Ten Commandments and God's other moral laws that are reiterated in the New Testament. God's Word is not outdated, and not even the smallest part of it is insignificant.

God inspired the writers of His Word as Paul makes plain: *All Scripture is inspired by God and is useful to teach us what is true and to make us realize what is wrong in our lives. It corrects us when we are wrong and teaches us to do what is right* (2 Timothy 3:16). Accepting its message produces new life through Jesus Christ by the forgiveness of our sins. The principles enable us to overcome temptations, as they did with Jesus. When tempted by Satan, He met each one with, "It is written."

God's Word is also relevant. Ignoring it has severe consequences, while obeying it leads to eternal life and God's blessings. Some prefer antinomianism (against the law). They want no rules, but if rules exist, they do not want to be held accountable for obeying them. Preferring, and even claiming, this philosophy does not make it possible. Whether or not we think God's Word is relevant is irrelevant. God proclaiming His Word relevant is enough to make it so.

God's Word reflects His character and shares His standards. Since He is the creator and the One we answer to, His Word is extremely pertinent.

Disregarding it and teaching others to follow suit makes us least in God's Kingdom. In fact, we will not enter the Kingdom. But obeying it and teaching others to do the same grants us a place in heaven. In the Great Commission, Jesus said, *Therefore, go and make disciples of all the nations, baptizing them in the name of the Father and the Son and the Holy Spirit. Teach these new disciples to obey all the commands I have given you. And be sure of this: I am with you always, even to the end of the age* (Matthew 28:19–20).

Real living is only achieved by loving, meditating, and adhering to the principles of God's holy Word. By pondering its principles and applying them to daily circumstances, our relationship with the Father is enhanced, and He is able to conform us to His Son's likeness.

CHAPTER FIVE

HANDLE YOUR ANGER; DON'T LET IT HANDLE YOU

MATTHEW 5:21–26

IF I FEEL ANGRY, AM I sinning? Or is it only sin if I hold on to the feeling for too long? Perhaps it's only sin when I allow the anger to form into an attitude of revenge. I want to repay the person for what they've done or said to me. But what about my anger over sinful actions people commit? Such as murder, theft, rape, sexual abuse, extortion, or emotional torment. Is anger in and of itself sin, or is it only sin when it goes awry?

When the news is bad, I have several choices, none of which are good: get angry, get anxious, or get frustrated. If I choose anger, I'll probably direct it toward God, since He's in charge of the circumstances. Choosing anxiety sets me up for physical and emotional problems. If I select frustration, I'll live each day with a sour attitude, and no one will want to associate with me.

According to Elisabeth Kubler-Ross, in her book, *On Death and Dying*, anger is the second stage of the grieving process. Surely, this anger over loss or at hearing devastating news couldn't be bad, could it?

In one of his sermons, Frederick Buechner told of a pre-teen who, in a fit of anger, secured a gun and shot his father. Although the father didn't die immediately, he did soon afterward. When the authorities asked the boy why he had shot his father, he told them because he could not stand his father. His father demanded too much of him, so he hated him.

Authorities placed the young boy in jail. Late one night, as the guard patrolled the corridor, he heard sounds coming from the boy's cell. He stopped to listen and heard the boy wailing, "I want my father; I want my father." But he couldn't get him back. He had killed him.

Anger is a God-created emotion, but one that, when unharnessed, can result in physical disease and even criminal actions. It's dangerous and personally destructive and affects our relationship with others and God. Anger can lead to judgmental attitudes, cause rifts between people, and hinder our ability to worship God effectively.

Anger in and of itself isn't a sin but a part of our natural makeup. Anger can become sin, however, if not correctly and quickly processed. Jesus became angry on at least two occasions when expelling Temple merchants who were cheating those bringing sacrifices (Mark 11 and John 2). And those who misinterpreted His law and bound others by their rigid rules certainly angered Him. Yet He didn't sin in His words, thoughts, or actions. How we handle anger determines whether it morphs into sin.

Numerous situations can produce anger if we allow them: someone cursing at us for no reason or talking about us behind our back, a spouse cheating, someone stealing something valuable from us, the boss firing us for an illegitimate reason or getting laid off, discovering someone flirting with our spouse, girlfriend, or boyfriend, or standing in line at a retail store behind someone who has thirty coupons—half of which are expired. Yet no one can make us angry. They can only create circumstances that make it easy for us to get angry. Becoming angry is, in the end, a personal choice.

Jesus now begins addressing negative issues like anger and, in doing so, further reveals how the religious authorities missed the law's intent. In their mind, simply obeying the sixth commandment not to kill kept one from being guilty of murder. Jesus crushed their expectations by teaching that anger and total disrespect for others made one just as guilty. We can kill a person's dignity and reputation with our words and actions.

Jesus' concern is with our heart, although He's concerned with our actions, also. Although Jesus is concerned with our actions, His chief concern is with our heart. The heart—or mind and emotions—is where actions and attitudes arise, but even sins of the mind alone are still sins. A person with premeditated intentions of murdering, but is prevented at the last moment by someone's unforeseen arrival, isn't innocent just because the intended act failed. In God's eyes, they are as guilty of murder as if they had perpetrated the actual crime.

Like any other damaging addiction, anger must be acknowledged and admitted. While this may appear an easy task, in reality it's not. Admitting anger runs contrary to our nature. No one enjoys admitting when they're wrong. More often than not, we choose to hold anger inside, allowing it to fester, which leads to physical, emotional, and spiritual harm and affects our relationships with others.

Why do we struggle with admitting anger? One reason is our mind's deceptive nature. We justify anger and thoughts of revenge by meditating on the injustice committed against us. While it's true that the nature of offenses might be severe, no wrong ever gives us sufficient reason for more than temporary anger as we process the hurt. And unforgiveness is never justified.

Pride also makes it easy to harbor anger. We don't enjoy admitting that we have faults or that we have contributed in some way to conflicts. We prefer the other party to admit wrong. Think of how many individuals commit crimes yet plead "Not guilty."

Anger contains a destructive nature. Since our bodies are temples of God's Spirit, anything that harms physically also does spiritually. Thoughts of revenge and feelings of hatred grieve God's Spirit and place us outside His will. Unprocessed anger hinders the flow of God's blessings, making us a spiritual mess.

The cure is admitting our anger to our self, God, and others when necessary. After all, God knows about our anger and often others do as well.

As we admit what is (anger) and what isn't (forgiveness), we open the path for God to take what isn't and bring it into reality.

Admitting anger is essential, but so is attempting to correct the injustice that led to it. Jesus addressed this aspect. Under the Old Testament system, sacrifices were atonements for sin designed to cover the guilt of the offender. They weren't substitutes because restitution was still required. These verses illustrate how unresolved anger affects our ability to worship God by placing a disconnect between the worshipper and the One worshipped. Unconfessed sin—anger in this case—interferes with worship. Religious acts will not clear a guilty conscience when forgiveness is withheld and attempts at reconciliation avoided.

The psalmist recognized sin's interference with his worship of God when he wrote, *If I had not confessed the sin in my heart, the Lord would not have listened* (Psalm 66:18). Injustices should be settled quickly when possible.

Reconciliation doesn't happen in every case, but we should make an attempt. Reconciliation should always be our goal. All parties in a conflict must be open to reconciliation for it to succeed, just as both spouses must agree to reconcile when one has betrayed the trust of the other.

Dealing with anger and correcting the conflict won't always avoid the consequences of actions arising out of our anger. Anger sometimes leads to murder. Repentance and sorrow over such an action doesn't mean a jury will declare the offender not guilty and excuse them from a jail sentence. The offender may even have to pay with their life. The more important element is that forgiveness has occurred—from God and hopefully from the offended party.

Paul also illustrates the importance of resolving angry conflicts quickly when he writes, *And "don't sin by letting anger control you." Don't let the sun go down while you are still angry* (Ephesians 4:26).

Only a transformed heart makes dealing adequately with anger possible. What we normally want is revenge—to get even for our hurt. When we hurt, we typically want to hurt others by inflicting pain on those who cause us pain and even on innocent bystanders.

Christ gives a new nature when we enter a relationship with him, but even this doesn't completely remove our struggle with sinful anger. Dealing with anger quickly involves a change of mind and ambition. Our inward change must be processed into outward actions. Only God can enable us to offer forgiveness instead of seeking revenge. We can do all things through the strength of Christ (Philippians 4:13), and letting go of anger when it's the easiest road is one of those things we can only do with God's help. Forgiveness is never easy, but it is the antidote for sinful anger and a step forward in living life as it really should be lived.

CHAPTER SIX

TRIUMPH OVER LUST

MATTHEW 5:27–30

WHEN HER SKIN TURNED YELLOW, her husband wasn't surprised. Cattie*
seemed to have it all. She married a preacher and planned to fulfill all the
wonderful roles that accompanied being a preacher's wife. For a while, things
went as she planned. The next six years passed quickly. Then one Sunday,
strangers visited the church. The next thing Cattie knew, she was packing for
a move.

Over the next five years, Cattie tired of being a preacher's wife and
convinced herself she had never wanted to be one in the first place. She found
a job in town and began hanging around with people who didn't share her
faith or her lifestyle.

Cattie's downward spiral began innocently enough: smoking. Then she
started drinking heavily and even buying alcohol for some of the teenagers
in the church. She changed her style of dress, wearing low-cut blouses and
short skirts. Sometimes, she wouldn't even come home at night but stayed in
sleazy motels instead.

Cattie's husband became suspicious. Eventually, the proof of her bad
habits surfaced. She admitted her addictions. Little did he know she was also
dabbling in drugs and having affairs with numerous men, one of which was
a church member.

Cattie's husband wasn't surprised when one day she said, "I don't love you anymore. I want a divorce." Nor was he surprised when she showed up to get the kids one day and was yellow all over. Her sexual escapades had rewarded her with Hepatitis.

Nathaniel Hawthorne's *The Scarlett Letter* also provides a timely example of unfaithfulness and how we can react to it. In part, the novel was an indictment against the Puritanical beliefs of Hawthorne's time. Hester Prynne lived in Amsterdam with her husband—a learned man and English by birth. He wanted to cross the ocean and live with those in Massachusetts, so he sent her ahead while he stayed to look after affairs.

Hester lived in Boston for two years, but her husband never arrived. Suddenly, she was pregnant, but the father remains a riddle. The evidence appeared to point to the preacher. Hester was pronounced guilty of adultery—a crime worthy of death. The town showed mercy by allowing her to live but sentenced her to stand on a platform where all could view her shame. Additionally, they required Hester to wear a mark of shame on her breast the remainder of her life—a scarlet "A."

Societies once condemned those who lived together before marriage, but the practice is now well-accepted by most. Sexual fidelity is threatened in most modern societies. Adultery—defined as sexual relationships between two people who are married but with someone other than their spouse—is common. As is fornication—sexual relationships between two unmarried individuals.

According to Jesus, lust in the heart makes one guilty of adultery or fornication, whether the actual act is perpetrated or not. Jesus touches on the subjects of sanctity and purity, both of which must be adhered to for successful marriages and real Christian living.

Just as with murder, the common belief was that avoiding the actual act of unfaithfulness relieved guilt. Jesus alludes to the seventh commandment forbidding adultery (Exodus 20:14). But more is involved than obedience to the law's letter. Lust invokes guilt whether we commit the sexual act or not.

Jesus does not condemn a passing glance or even admiring the beauty of another person. In fact, physical traits typically initiate relationships with the opposite sex, but the relationship must quickly add other foundations or it will crumble almost as soon as it begins.

Lust is a foreboding issue. If we lust in our hearts after another person, then we are guilty of unfaithfulness to whomever we are in a relationship with. Once again, Jesus goes to the heart of the matter. Lust is as powerful an emotion as anger is. A "Beware of the Dog" sign issues a strong caution, and Jesus does likewise with His warning against lust. A small amount can soon grow to large proportions, which can lead to fornication, adultery, pornography, and other spiritually unhealthy means of satisfying the normal sexual drive God has created in us.

Everyone deals with lust at some point. While God permits—and expects—the passing glance—the second glance, the stare, and the resulting thoughts get us into trouble. Our thoughts lead to feelings, which in turn result in actions. Jesus' warning is not a directive to think sex is evil or sinful. Nor is He promoting a life of celibacy. Sex is God's creation and proper within marital relationships for enjoyment and for procreation.

What God wants is for us to have a godly and proper view of sex. Sadly, it has taken an eruption of sexually transmitted diseases to make people think about loose sexual living. The consequences of the 1960s and 1970s sexual revolution are still cropping up. While believers should provide the example of God's sexual standards, research shows they are no more obedient in this area than unbelievers. Christian teens and young adults have sexual relationships outside the marriage covenant at about the same rate as those unengaged with churches. Real Christian living means taking this teaching and our example into our schools, society, government, and health care centers.

An old saying—but one that still holds true—is that "sex sells." Scantily dressed men, women, and even children are used to promote many things. Distortions of God's plan for sexual relationships are viewed on television, heard on the radio, and watched on the Internet and at movies. Sex sells, and advertisers make full use of it.

Hedonism makes pleasure the chief goal of life, and sex is viewed as a part of this pleasure. The result is a breakdown in marriages and relationships. But the cure is not physical escapism, forced celibacy, or physical mutilation. Origen, an early church father, had himself castrated after reading this passage, but even such extreme measures cannot remove the temptation. Monks and nuns have discovered this as well as those who work in church traditions that forbid their leaders to marry.

Dealing with distorted teachings and practices about sexual relationships involves dealing with the initial lustful desire. The cure is not refraining from the physical act, although this is involved, too. Nor will giving into the desire solve the issue. Being unfaithful is a temporary fix to lust. Our desire will return just as an addict's does. We must deal with the desire and learn to control it.

Looking at members of the opposite sex is not the problem. Not looking would remove a part of our humanity that God has created for a purpose. The type of look is the issue. A wrong look is an inappropriate, intentional, and repeated gaze with intentions or desires to go beyond the look—whether with actions or just in the imagination, which is an expression of our hearts. Rather than the lustful looking leading to sin, it is actually our sinful thoughts that lead to lustful looking.

Believers aren't immune to lust and need to take Jesus' warning seriously. The temptation is not the sin; how we respond determines this. David didn't sin by seeing Bathsheba bathing (2 Samuel 11). He sinned when he continued to look and by what he chose to do after the passing glance.

When the temptation to lust is present, only God can help us deal with and overcome the desire.

Some practical steps can help us avoid situations wherein we might be tempted. We can run from unavoidable situations. Joseph did this with Potiphar's wife. He was a servant in her house and had no choice in being there, but he did have a choice about having sex with her (Genesis 39).

Praying in advance for God's strength is also helpful. We cannot reason ourselves out of these situations after our emotions take over. What unmarried couple sits in an apartment room and reasons out the advantages and disadvantages of having sex? A part of advance preparation is dressing daily in God's armor (Ephesians 6:10–18).

An old proverb says, "Sow a thought and reap an act. Sow an act and reap a habit. Sow a habit and reap a character. Sow a character and reap a destiny."

Jesus, when He appeals to our hands and eyes, uses figurative language to help us deal with the issues that cause us more susceptibility to temptation. The right side symbolizes our best and most precious faculties. It refers to the side of precedence and strength. He is not speaking of literal mutilation to keep us from lusting but rather severing our sinful impulses. We should give up the best we have if it causes us to succumb to temptation.

Involved in avoiding what we've determined not to do is staying away from situations enhancing the temptation. When we decide not to do something—whether sinful or just unhealthy—we must use our good sense and stay away from situations where that particular thing will tempt us.

Adultery and fornication may be mutually enjoyable, but God classifies them as sin. As is any unfaithfulness to God. One of God's favorite pictures when rebuking His people's unfaithfulness to Him in the Old Testament was the marital relationship with its adherent faithfulness. He often compared faithfulness to fidelity and unfaithfulness to adultery and fornication.

Believers can't enjoy inappropriate sexual relationships and real living simultaneously. But there is deliverance from this and any other sin. We receive a new mind after accepting Christ's forgiveness, along with the ability to know Christ's mind. Our new ways of thinking transfer into better ways of acting. We look at situations with renewed vision. Surrendering to this new nature helps deal with sexual temptation, just as it does with any temptation to disobey God's principles.

I recall the conversation I had with my daughter concerning her commitments to refrain from certain actions, sexual unfaithfulness among them. I advised her to stay away from situations where the temptation to compromise her convictions would be present. Making such decisions as teenagers or adults labels us as counter-cultural. Our commitments take us against the grain of society as a whole.

Parents have the responsibility of talking to their children and teens about purity in sexual relationships. If they don't, they will get their information from friends, peers, and significant others. And the messages will often contradict God's Word.

Believers are prisoners of the Lord (Ephesians 5:3), and our bodies are temples of His Spirit (1 Corinthians 6:19–20). Our bodies, minds, and emotions all belong to Him, and we are to guard their purity.

No person or thing other than Christ can completely satisfy us. Our greatest love is not to be for another person, but rather for God foremost, and then our neighbor. Loving God with all our being and others as ourselves makes temptation—including sexual impurity—easier to overcome. It also leads us to real Christian living.

*Name changed to protect privacy.

CHAPTER SEVEN

HAVE A HEALTHY MARRIAGE

MATTHEW 5:27–32

MAINTAINING A MARRIAGE AND FAMILY takes hard work and a lot of maintenance. The statistics on successful marriages remain steady, as they have for many years: only about half survive divorce. Even fewer survive a second go-round and still less a third. The third time is not always a charm.

As the townspeople punished Hester Prynne by requiring her to wear an "A" on her breast in Hawthorne's *The Scarlet Letter*, we're often tempted to label divorced persons with a "D." On the heels of His warning about lust, Jesus addresses divorce. While some societies aren't as cruel as they once were to divorcees, it continues—even if in subtle ways—to make them feel as if they are second-class citizens. This is often truer in churches than anywhere else. A divorce label can affect a person's ability to borrow money or work in some professions.

Regardless of who's at fault—and in many instances a little fault lies with both parties—divorce carries devastating effects for all involved, especially children. Effects can include psychiatric problems, health changes, depression, and impoverished economic conditions. Children can experience social, behavioral, emotional, and academic problems—often believing they're responsible for their parent's breakup.

Complicating matters are the conflicting views believers within and between denominations have about divorce: it's not permissible for any reason, it's permissible under any circumstances, it's permissible in some cases (unfaithfulness, abuse, an unbelieving spouse's desertion), but remarriage is forbidden, or divorce and remarriage are both permissible under certain circumstances.

Jesus mentions unfaithfulness as a permissible reason for divorce (Matthew 5:32), and Paul addresses unbelieving spouses leaving believing partners as another permissible reason (1 Corinthians 7:15).

But more importantly, what does it take to solidify a Christian marriage and what are God's purposes for it? To understand divorce, we must understand marriage. God performed the first marriage between Adam and Eve in the Garden of Eden. As Adam looked over and named the animals, he noticed none resembled him.

God noticed Adam's loneliness, put him in a deep sleep, took a rib, and made him a helper: woman. When Adam saw her, he remarked, *This one is bone from my bone, and flesh from my flesh! She will be called "woman," because she was taken from "man"* (Genesis 2:23). After performing their wedding ceremony, God said, *This explains why a man leaves his father and mother and is joined to his wife, and the two are united into one* (Genesis 2:24).

Marriage isn't a human arrangement but a God idea. Most weddings call attention to this with a familiar opening statement: "Dearly beloved, we are assembled here in the presence of God, to join this man and this woman in holy matrimony, which is instituted by God." While a clear indication of God's involvement, the further challenge for the married couple is to continue involving God after the ceremony and to honor Him for bringing them together.

God does not command marriage but offers it as a choice. Nevertheless, when two people decide to marry, God becomes a necessary element if the marriage has any chance of surviving in the manner God designs. Many single men and women have been the brunt of well-meaning people desiring to "set them up"—people who don't understand that being single is not disobedience to God's commands. These sincere individuals often overlook that God grants some the gift of singleness—a lifestyle that has merit. Single people have more time to serve God (1 Corinthians 7:7). While natural for men and women to be attracted to one another, remaining single is not abnormal if this is God's plan for a person.

Generally speaking, boys and girls grow up, fall in love, marry, and populate the earth. Procreation is a major part of God's plan as viewed in His instructions to Adam and Eve: *Be fruitful and multiply. Fill the earth and govern it. Reign over the fish in the sea, the birds in the sky, and all the animals that scurry along the ground* (Genesis 1:28). God designs acts of sex for pleasure and procreation, but this is only permitted within the marriage union. Such a conclusion is almost a lost philosophy in many modern societies.

Loose views of marriage and sexual relationships have almost destroyed the divine nature of the institution. Divorce rates are high, living together before marriage is common, sex before marriage is prevalent, and unfaithfulness within marriages is all too common.

Successful marriages require hard work by determined individuals who recognize its divine nature and are willing to obey God's guidelines. Although marriages between believers and unbelievers can succeed, the challenge is even greater. In religiously mixed marriages, the believer must work diligently to establish a godly influence in the home, often without support from the unbelieving spouse. In some cases, the unbelieving partner is even antagonistic.

Jesus said of marriage, *"Haven't you read the Scriptures? . . . They record that from the beginning 'God made them male and female.'" And he said, "'This explains why a man leaves his father and mother and is joined to his wife, and the two are united into one.' Since they are no longer two but one, let no one split apart what God has joined together"* (Matthew 19:4–6).

While sacred, marriage is not a sacrament. One can experience God's grace through marriage, but it has no relationship with saving grace. Marriage neither adds nor subtracts from a person's spiritual journey toward salvation. An unbelieving spouse is not saved through marriage to a believing spouse. At the same time, marriage is more than a civil or social arrangement between two individuals. Marriages should be treated as holy and sacred and never in derogatory ways. Spouses are not "old ladies," "old men," or "balls and chain."

While books, seminars, and retreats can enhance marriages, only one ideal manual for successful marriages exists: the Bible. Here we discover that marriage is more than two people deciding to live together, share the same house, and have children. It is more than meals and sex together. Marriage is even more than showing and receiving love. Marriage is a union best represented in the marriage ceremony by the couple's vows and with a "unity" symbol of some type.

Marriage is a union of body, soul, and spirit. According to Scripture, the couple becomes one flesh. Two whole persons become one, although neither loses their identity or personality. From a legal standpoint, marriage is two people united in a sexual relationship which consummates the marriage.

Although sexual encounters are a regular part of healthy marriages, marriages based on attraction or even sex alone are doomed. The soul is not our sexual side but rather involves intellect and emotion. Couples are joined in a sexual, intellectual, and emotional union. Common interests are vital as well as a shared vision for the future. When two believers marry, their spirits also unite because they share the same faith and worship the same Lord.

Perhaps most importantly is a marriage's reflection of the relationship between Christ and His church. Marriage illustrates how God joins Himself to us through a faith relationship. Paul explained this in his epistle to the Ephesians. After instructing wives to submit to their husbands and husbands to love their wives, he said; *This is a great mystery, but it is an illustration of the way Christ and the church are one* (Ephesians 5:32).

A part of really living life is realizing our marriages exemplify our relationship with Christ. We also understand how our marriages can lead others to encounter Christ.

CHAPTER EIGHT

SAY WORDS THAT MEAN SOMETHING

MATTHEW 5:33–37

TRUTH IS SOMETIMES DIFFICULT TO find. People once prided themselves in being as good as their word, and fortunately, some still do. Although presently common and even mandatory, written contracts weren't always necessary. Attempt to purchase a home, vehicle, or major appliance and tell the salesperson, "Don't worry about it. I'll pay you," and note the reaction. Contracts are necessary because of a credibility gap, but they also serve as contemporary forms of oaths.

My paternal grandfather prided himself in having a good name when it came to borrowing money. In his words, he often had "to rob Peter to pay Paul." Although I'm sure he still had to sign at least one form, the loan officer never did a credit check to determine whether or not he would loan my grandfather the money. Paperwork was merely a formality. The loan was guaranteed because of my grandfather's good name.

Our name is important because of what people associate with it. Good parents will teach their children the importance of a good reputation and warn them against ruining it. I remember an aunt who engaged a man to cut trees on her property and made only a verbal agreement with him. He arrived, cut the trees, and left. Only later did she realize he had duped her.

With no contract and no idea how to locate him, she lost a large sum of money in timber.

Paul Harvey told a story about four high school boys who arrived late to their morning class. They informed the teacher they had had a flat tire. Although they missed a test, she told them they could make it up. She gave them paper and pencil and sent each one to a different corner of the room. They would pass if they gave the same answer to one question; "Which tire was flat?"

Some people have professions that, over time, have led them to be suspect: used car salesmen, preachers, lawyers, and politicians. Closer to home is the temptation to falsify an income tax return or plagiarize by copying work from the Internet rather than doing it ourselves. Daniel Webster said, "There is nothing so powerful as truth—and often nothing so strange." Jewish rabbis thought lying was one of the four great sins that would keep a person out of God's presence.

In Jesus' day, truth was revered but buried under a heap of tradition. God's law was lowered to the people's level, making it appear that they obeyed it when they really didn't. In American courts, the importance of truthful testimony is reflected in what witnesses are asked: "Do you swear to tell the truth, the whole truth, and nothing but the truth, so help you God?" The highest code of truth, however, lies within God's court. Just living lets us handle the truth carelessly, but real living requires us to adhere to truth deliberately and consistently.

Old Testament teaching on truth was scattered but always warned against perjuring or wearing falsely. When an oath was made, something or someone's name was added for credibility, similar to putting up collateral to guarantee a loan, and then a legally binding document was signed. If a religious oath was made, God's name was used. A corruption of the seriousness of this practice is still heard when someone remarks, "I swear to God." Oaths were designed to reflect absolute truth.

God allowed people to use His name when making oaths or promises. When Abraham sent his servant Eliezer back to his homeland to secure a bride for his son, Isaac, he required him to swear by God's name that he would not go find a wife from the pagan people (Genesis 24:3). When Jonathan agreed to protect David from his father's attempt to kill him, he used God's name in the covenant: *So Jonathan made a solemn pact with David, saying, "May the LORD destroy all your enemies"* (1 Samuel 20:16).

God Himself sometimes made oaths using His name. After Abraham demonstrated his willingness to give up his promised son when God asked him to, God said, *I swear by my own name that I will certainly bless you. I will multiply your descendants beyond number, like the stars in the sky and the sand on the seashore. Your descendants will conquer the cities of their enemies* (Genesis 22:16–17).

Just as God accommodated in the matter of divorce, so He does in making oaths. God knows we are prone to deceit and lying. Had the propensity been toward honesty, He would not have needed to make the provisions for promises. Promises increase the motivation to tell the truth just as contracts motivate us to perform jobs or pay our debts.

But promises are only as reliable as the people who make them. Peter denied with an oath he was with Jesus, but his oath didn't make his words true (Luke 22:60). Our promises can be unreliable and also rash. Jephthah—a judge in Israel who advanced against his enemies, the Ammonites—said, *If you give me victory over the Ammonites, I will give to the LORD whatever comes out of my house to meet me when I return in triumph. I will sacrifice it as a burnt offering* (Judges 11:30–31). Unfortunately, his daughter was the first to greet him.

Like many of God's laws, the one concerning promises was perverted. The emphasis was placed in the wrong place, with the missing ingredient being the proper and serious circumstances necessary to make vows in the first place.

The perversion of our promises comes when we take them lightly, thereby making them meaningless. When we make them and then break them without thinking, others will cease to believe us—similar to saying "I'm sorry" and continuing to do the same thing over and over. Or like the little boy who cried wolf continually when there wasn't one. When the wolf actually came, no one believed him anymore. Instead of a mark of honesty, our word becomes a mark of deceit.

By Jesus' time, rabbinical standards had lowered God's standards to the level that dishonesty was allowed when making promises, unless that promise mentioned God. Truth, however, is objective, not subjective or determined by individuals. Nor does it vary between individuals. Truth is based on God's Word and does not change from generation to generation. Without objective truth, no standard exists by which to judge our actions. Truth is what God says, not what we believe or accept.

From Jesus' perspective—which is the only one that matters—we should mean what we say and speak the truth. When our word is dependable, we don't need promises, oaths, or vows—although we might be required to make them in certain situations. People will recognize us as being as good as our word.

When there is complete truthfulness in our thoughts, words, and actions, our promises will mean something, and we will have taken one step further toward real living.

CHAPTER NINE

GIVE UP YOUR RIGHTS

MATTHEW 5:38–42

ON MAY 10, 1775, THE Second Continental Congress met in Philadelphia, Pennsylvania. Although they possessed no legal authority, they had to make decisions because of military events transpiring between the American colonists and the British. By the end of 1775, independence was almost inevitable because of the colonial mistrust of the entire British society.

In January 1776, news arrived that the British were sending German troops. Thomas Paine, an English pamphleteer, called for complete independence. Congress appointed a committee to justify independence and asked the youngest member, Thomas Jefferson, to prepare a draft. His statement has inspired oppressed people for hundreds of years: "We hold these truths to be self-evident, that all men are created equal, that they are endowed by their Creator with certain unalienable Rights, that among these are Life, Liberty, and the pursuit of Happiness. That to secure these rights, Governments are instituted among Men, deriving their just powers from the consent of the governed, That whenever any Form of Government becomes destructive of these ends, it is the Right of the People to alter or to abolish it, and to institute new Government."

Since this time, people's rights have continued to expand. During the 1950s and 1960s, the United States of America experienced various civil rights movements, including those for African Americans, women, labor unions, children, prisoners, homosexuals, and abortion activists.

We live in a time when people are overly concerned with our rights and privileges and will go to great lengths to protect them. This is a natural tendency of the sinful nature we are born with and continue to fight with even after we trust Christ as our Savior. We want revenge against those who infringe on our rights and are quite satisfied to retaliate in numerous ways. When this is our chief concern, anything getting in the way becomes disposable, often leading us to trample on other's rights in the process. When we are too concerned with self, no room exists for our concern about others.

Real living, however, realizes self cannot be number one. We must love God supremely and others as ourselves and also be willing to give up whatever it takes to demonstrate Christ's love. Pedestals are for placing others on, not ourselves.

These words of Jesus are frequently misinterpreted and misapplied and have been used to support pacifism, conscientious objection, lawlessness, and anarchy. But instead of focusing on rights we have, Jesus shares rights we should give up so we can experience life as He wants us to.

Retaliation is the first right we should be willing to relinquish. Jesus refers to the Old Testament principle of an eye for an eye and a tooth for a tooth (Exodus 21:24). Termed the principle of *lex talionis*, it teaches the punishment should match the crime exactly. But the purpose wasn't to advocate revenge. Rather, the law served as a deterrent to curtail further crime and also to prevent excessive punishment. When we are bent on personal vengeance and angry retaliation, we are often tempted to exact more punishment than the crime merits.

In contrast, Jesus says not to resist the one harming us. He is not teaching that we shouldn't take a stand against evil, but is speaking about personal retaliation. Both Dr. Martin Luther King, Jr. in America and Mahatma Gandhi in India used this teaching to instruct their followers in the art of peaceful demonstrations for the rights of the oppressed in their respective countries.

When others wrong us, we are tempted to retaliate, forgetting that vengeance belongs to God. God's standard is *If your enemies are hungry, give them food to eat. If they are thirsty, give them water to drink. You will heap burning coals of shame on their heads, and theLORD will reward you* (Proverbs 25:21–22).

Jesus' statement does not mean we should ignore evil. Our mandate involves resisting evil in both our personal lives and the world. We have God's armor to fight personal evil (Ephesians 6) and our collective influence to do so worldwide. Jesus is referring to evil people who harm us personally. Vengeful retaliation should not be our response. Rather we overcome someone's evil toward us with good.

Nor does Jesus insinuate that we don't have the right to be treated with dignity, respect, and consideration. Being God's creations gives us these things. The emphasis is on our reaction when mistreated. As difficult as it is, we must turn the other cheek. In Jewish society, slapping was the most demeaning and contemptuous thing someone could do. It attacked a person's honor and was a terrible indignity. Turning the other cheek means we possess a non-avenging, non-retaliatory, humble, and gentle spirit.

Jesus teaches what He models. He confronted evil actions toward others, but He also allowed Himself to be mistreated and abused. Peter writes of Him, *He did not retaliate when he was insulted, nor threaten revenge when he suffered* (1 Peter 2:23).

Real living means giving up our right to vengeful retaliation when personally insulted. We are not required to forego the law's protection when we have no other recourse, but we must be satisfied with what the law determines fits the crime. The danger in breaking Jesus' instruction comes when believers take each other to court instead of settling our differences among ourselves. Doing so damages Christianity's reputation and ruins the testimony of unity we strive so show. Paul was appalled when he heard of believers in Corinth doing this (1 Corinthians 6:1–8).

A second right entails security. The tunic was a type of undergarment while the coat was an outer garment that also served as a blanket. Since the person is suing, Jesus references a person having legitimate claims to these objects. The more important issue is our willingness to give up what makes us feel secure if it prevents hard feelings from developing. If our mistakes lead to legal action against us, we should be willing to go beyond the fair legal agreement to show our regret. Doing this also demonstrates that we don't have bitter or resentful feelings. Better to be defrauded than to have and show a spiteful revengeful spirit.

So often, the things we normally associate with security don't bring it—such as homes, autos, clothes, food, retirement, and insurance policies. Since the Lord gives everything we have, we do not have to guard it with jealousy. Our right to security is worth sacrificing if it honors God. We can trust God to take care of us.

Two further rights we must be willing to surrender are time and money. God's original plan was freedom for everyone. He created no one in slavery. Yet, history and present circumstances show many instances of it and other limits placed on individuals. According to Roman law, a soldier could force a civilian to carry his pack one mile. This forced servitude inconvenienced the individual, who had to carry items for the oppressors they hated. Soldiers forced Simon of Cyrene to carry Jesus' cross (Matthew 27:32).

Time is a precious commodity. We all have the same amount but choose to use it in various pursuits. We should give up our right of time when asked, especially when doing so impacts God's Kingdom. We should not resent it when others ask us to do things that take our time. If possible, we should accommodate them with a cheerful heart, knowing God is observing and possibly sending the opportunity.

Additionally, we willingly give up our right to money and property. Such a sacrifice is made easier when we remember that everything we have belongs to God and is given to us by him. Helping those with genuine needs allows us to serve God by serving them. When we do it quickly and generously, it enhances our testimony. John writes, *If someone has enough money to live well and sees a brother or sister in need but shows no compassion—how can God's love be in that person* (1 John 3:17)?

When we realize that life is not about us, that everything we have comes from God, and that nothing comes our way except what is passed through the Father's hand, it is easier to give up rights we believe we have to further the love of Christ. This attitude transports us into the field of real living.

CHAPTER TEN

LOVE YOUR ENEMIES

MATTHEW 5:43–48

IMAGINE A LIFEGUARD HOVERING OVER a pool of lively swimmers. Suddenly calls erupt, and he spots someone lashing about in the deep end. If the drowning person was the lifeguard's close friend or a casual acquaintance, he would probably dive in without thinking. But assume the drowning person was a contemptible person or an enemy; someone who had wronged the lifeguard, committed an injustice against him, cheated him, or stabbed him in the back. Even worse, what if the lifeguard knows the person is a murderer, child abuser, or addict? Would he lunge in with the same immediacy—or even at all?

Paul mentioned how scarce the type of love Jesus commands is when he wrote, *Now, most people would not be willing to die for an upright person, though someone might perhaps be willing to die for a person who is especially good* (Romans 5:7). Jesus wants us to risk loving people regardless of who they are or what they've done. That is difficult, but necessary if we are to enjoy real Christian living.

This is perhaps the heart of Jesus' Sermon on the Mount since it contrasts true and false righteousness and real versus play religion. It takes us down to the nitty-gritty of love and the sacrifice required to show it regardless of whether we experience it in return or not. Jesus begins by reminding the people that they had been taught to love their neighbors and hate their enemies. But God had not taught them that.

According to the Old Testament, loving one's neighbor involved going so far as to return a lost animal even if it belonged to an enemy (Deuteronomy 22:1–3). A neighbor was anyone in need, but the religious leaders changed God's standard by teaching people to love only those they got along with. Enemies should be hated. The religious leaders also conveniently omitted the phrase "as yourself." Since they were extremely self centered, they couldn't imagine loving someone as much as they loved themselves. Neighbor was narrowed to mean only preferred or approved of individuals, and the only people they sanctioned were people like them. They also added the phrase "hate your enemy," and anyone not an Israelite belonged in the hated category. This type of pride led to extreme hatred of the Gentiles.

Jesus restored God's original intention by teaching love rather than hate for enemies. Just as He responded to people without discrimination, so should we. This is the most powerful teaching on love and was a command that must have appeared foolish and naïve to the religious leaders who were proud, prejudiced, hateful, and judgmental. Jesus called them hypocrites. We often make the same mistakes by basing our love on the desirability of an object, by only loving those we desire to imitate, or by only loving those we know will love us back. This type of love requires small sacrifice and little effort.

The Bible references several kinds of love: *storge*, which refers to natural affection; *philia*, which is friendship love; *eros* which is sexual love; and *agapē*, which is unconditional love. Jesus speaks of *agapē*—a love involving action. God possesses this type of love and proved it by allowing Jesus to die for us while we were still in our sin: *But God showed his great love for us by sending Christ to die for us while we were still sinners* (Romans 5:8).

Rather than questioning whom to love, our concern should be how to love most helpfully. People can be mean, slanderous, abusive, and judgmental, but we must respond with love.

Along with loving our enemies, we must also pray for them. As Jesus was persecuted by those who rejected Him and His message, so will we be as His representatives. When this happens, we should pray for those doing it. We should pray for them to seek forgiveness and God's grace. Jesus even prayed for those crucifying Him (Luke 23:34). Imitating His actions demonstrates God's agape love.

German Lutheran pastor and theologian Dietrich Bonhoeffer said of this teaching, "This is the supreme demand. Through the medium of prayer we go to our enemy, stand by his side, and plead for him to God."

By loving and praying for our enemies, we demonstrate our relationship with Christ. This abnormal behavior will label us cross-cultural, but prove our distinctiveness. Christians are often charged with failing to live up to our name, but showing impartial love, whether people deserve it or not, makes others sit up and take notice.

A Christian doctor and Navajo nurses once nurtured a poor Navajo woman back to health. Her people had cast her out when they thought she was dying. The doctor and nurses found her after she had endured several days of exposure and carried her to the hospital, where she received nine weeks of excellent care. After she had healed, she remarked to the nurse, "Why did the doctor do all that for me? He is a white man, and I am an Indian. I never heard of anything like this before." The Navajo nurse, who was a Christian, said, "You know, it is the love of Christ that made him do that." Several weeks later, the nurses encouraged her to believe in Christ. As she thought about this decision, the doctor entered. The woman's face lit up, and she said, "If Jesus is anything like the doctor, I can trust Him forever."

Loving and praying for our enemies—though challenging—illustrates a wonderful testimony of real living.

CHAPTER ELEVEN

MAKE A GOOD INVESTMENT

MATTHEW 6:1–4

GOOD INVESTMENTS REQUIRE PATIENCE. THOSE who choose to invest money in stocks, bonds, and mutual bonds must be willing to ride out the roller-coaster ups and downs of the stock market. Taking money out when the market is down often means losing money due to fees for early withdrawals. Although money might be lost on a downward spiral, the upward trends normally outnumber the downward rides. Being patient and resisting the urge to jump ship usually results in making money over the long haul. Anytime we seek to invest, we will probably come across the following disclaimer: "Past success does not guarantee future performance."

One of the most significant events of the late nineteenth century was urban and city growth resulting from immigrants and those from rural areas pouring in. They could enjoy better education and culture in urban areas by attending theaters, museums, and art galleries. Although an exciting time, the influx brought many problems to city life; transportation and healthcare were inadequate, slums developed, and crime escalated.

But out of these unhealthy circumstances, churches responded with giving spirits. The social gospel gained momentum, and people demonstrated concern for the poor. Churches provided food and homes for the indigent. D. L. Moody founded mission schools. The Young Men's Christian Association (YMCA) and Young Women's Christian Association (YWCA) made religion a wholesome recreation, along with providing study classes and musicals. William Booth, a Methodist minister who wanted to reach the poor by open-air evangelism and social work, founded the Salvation Army.

In these verses, Jesus encourages a giving spirit and pronounces it a requirement for real living. While some maintain this type of spirit naturally flows from our innate goodness—our "better angels"—it is only a by-product of a relationship with Christ. By nature, we are stingy. Two young children playing together are more likely to fight over their toys than share them.

Maintaining the natural stinginess of people doesn't imply unbelievers don't ever give or give with honorable motives. Rather, giving apart from a relationship with Christ is normally infrequent and often motivated by dishonorable ulterior motives.

Before Christ, homes for orphans, the sick, and the indigent were non-existent even though the world was filled with toil, poverty, and slavery. Great poverty lived side by side with great affluence. The situation after Christ's arrival differed. His sacrificial love, and that of His followers, made an enduring impact. Hospitals, better care for the poor, reform laws for women and other minorities, labor laws, and the abolition of slavery are all examples of how Christ's love and giving—and that of His followers—have continued to impact the world.

Prior to Christ, Judaism incorporated a strong concern for charity. People gave alms, but the act was viewed primarily as a duty. Following Christ's arrival, the motives for giving began to change. Giving would proceed from adopting the principles of God's divine love rather than from a mindset of mere duty.

Real Christian giving comes from the total surrender to God's authority in our life. When it doesn't, giving becomes hypocritical, like religion without a relationship. We can give because of a guilty conscience, or because we want to impress a person or group of people. We may even give large sums at the end of a fiscal year so we can decrease our tax responsibility. If we are not careful, our giving can be nothing more than pretense or show.

Cain is an early Biblical example of giving that doesn't proceed from surrender. He and his brother Abel brought offerings to God. Abel's fat portions from the firstborn of his flock were accepted, but Cain's fruit of the soil was not (Genesis 4:3-7). God's rejection had nothing to do with Cain's sacrifice not containing blood, but everything to do with his wrong attitude. When his hypocrisy was exposed, he murdered his brother (Genesis 4:8).

Ananias and Sapphira are another example (Acts 5:1-11). Some believers sold property and brought the proceeds to the apostles. Ananias followed suit, claiming he had brought the entire proceeds when, in fact, he retained a portion of the funds. His mistake was telling the apostles he brought the entire sum. Ananias wasn't required to give it all, but he lied when he claimed he did. Sapphira went along with the deception, and they both died.

Giving for show doesn't proceed from a heart surrendered to God. Rather, it magnifies the person instead of God. And the only reward is praise from others. Giving in this way is hypocritical—a root word originally referring to a Greek actor wearing a mask to portray a role. The term came to refer to someone pretending to be something they weren't.

The Philippian Christians, on the other hand, provide an example of surrendered giving. They first gave because they loved Paul, their father in the faith. When he departed for Thessalonica, they sent messengers to see how he was doing, then took a collection to meet his financial needs. They even gave a second time and then throughout Paul's lifetime.

When the church council gathered at Jerusalem, they asked Paul to request money from the Gentiles. The believers at Philippi competed for the chance to help the Jews. Paul records their response: *They even did more than we had hoped, for their first action was to give themselves to the Lord and to us, just as God wanted them to do* (2 Corinthians 8:5).

Surrendered giving realizes giving is a sacrificial investment in God's work that has no connection with how much we have. Giving material possessions with this attitude results in spiritual blessings. The amount or what form is determined by us, but should be in proportion to the magnanimity of the needs we are aware of. Such giving demonstrates love in the truest sense.

John Wanamaker once made a trip to China to see how his mission money was being used. As he traveled through the country, he came upon an old farmer plowing with a crude instrument. The plow was drawn by an ox alongside a young man. Out of curiosity, Wanamaker asked for an explanation. The man explained that the chapel down the road needed a steeple so the church could be seen from miles around. The members prayed about the matter but just did not have enough money. The man's son had said, "Let us sell one of our oxen, and I will take the yoke of the ox we sell." In response to the explanation, Wanamaker prayed, "Lord, let me be hitched to a plow, so that I may know the joy of sacrificial giving."

When giving with the proper motives and from a surrendered heart, we are more concerned with spiritual rewards than material profits. When giving to please others or placate guilt feelings, the only rewards we gain are from others.

Paul's principle of sowing and reaping applies to giving: *Don't be misled— you cannot mock the justice of God. You will always harvest what you plant* (Galatians 6:7). While normally applied to wrong actions and thoughts, this principle also applies when giving our money. Spending on sinful or selfish pleasures can lead to loss of money and destruction of our bodies while spending it on spiritual work garners spiritual blessings. Nor does money spent on the body have any lasting, eternal fruit. But money spent on God's work brings blessings now and in eternity.

Our challenge is not to give up doing good through our giving. The task of responding to burdens can be . . . burdensome. Poor people, hurting people, natural disasters, and tragedies will always exist, but we must continue giving, knowing God will reward our efforts. Giving should be based on our surrender to God and our love for others, not because we think God will accept us because we give.

Surrendered giving, by its nature, is sacrificial and seeks practical ways to share our goods, money, and acts of goodwill. Good intentions and warm feelings aren't enough. Fulfillment comes by knowing God delights in our acts of mercy. Giving that proceeds from a surrendered life searches for creative ways to give by doing more than throwing money at projects and needs. Regardless of when or how much we invest, it should be regular, systematic, and real.

CHAPTER TWELVE

PRAY EFFECTIVELY

MATTHEW 6:5-15

I GREW UP BELIEVING PRAYER was a normal part of a believer's life. My family always prayed before our meals, and Dad encouraged me to say my prayers each night before I went to bed. Dad also said a prayer when we finished our family devotion. I watched people pray several times when I attended church: in Sunday school, at the beginning of the service, before the offering was taken, and at the end of the worship service.

Any teaching on prayer necessarily involves confusion and questions but is vital for real Christian living. For some, majoring on God's sovereignty alleviates the need for prayer altogether, while others who major on human freedom believe everything depends on prayer. Some propose prayer is lining up with what God has already determined to do, while others maintain it is asking God to do what He otherwise wouldn't do.

Most of us probably fall somewhere in the middle of the two above extremes—believing God sovereignly controls but also maintaining He responds to our prayers. Scripture seems to support this view by proclaiming God's control but also telling believers to ask. All this makes the elements surrounding prayer somewhat confusing.

Although different conclusions and ideas about prayer abound, it's clear we'll miss real Christian living without it. However, one thing is certain: our prayers are directed to God. While it seems basic to say we should pray to God, not all prayers are directed that way. Jesus tells a story about a proud Pharisee and hated tax collector and concludes the Pharisee prayed to himself (Luke 18:11).

The religion of Judaism placed a high priority on prayer, but rabbinical teachings and ritualization had corrupted many of the people's prayers. Some merely read their prayers, and others repeated prayers from memory. Faithful Jews repeated the Shema (Deuteronomy 6:4–9) in the morning and at night. They also prayed the Shemoneh (a formalized prayer containing eighteen prayers for various occasions) in the morning, the afternoon, and the evening. Prayers existed for every object and occasion, and some were quite lengthy. Additionally, many who offered prayers did so with indifference and pride, desiring only to be seen and heard by their fellow Jews.

We avoid these mistakes by addressing our prayers to God and with the proper attitude. For the believer, prayer brings us into the presence of the only God who stands ready to answer. Our prayers need focus, and a quiet place for offering, since our minds tend to wander. We can find ourselves thinking about family, friends, and the day's activities—and worrying about all three. Having a focused daily time for prayer does not negate the validity of "microwave" prayers—those short prayers we say during the day when we need God to intervene in our situation. Paul tells us to pray without ceasing (1 Thessalonians 5:17).

Nonbelievers often view prayer as wish fulfillment or wishful thinking. Believers fall into the same trap when we have a wrong understanding and perspective of prayer. Our prayers should be more than a wish list—and more outward focused than inwardly directed. When said selflessly, our prayers will seek God's plan in personal, local, and world matters.

Prayer is directed to God in Jesus' name. He grants access when we come accepting His atoning death. The writer of Hebrews says, *And so, dear brothers and sisters, we can boldly enter heaven's Most Holy Place because of the blood of Jesus. By his death, Jesus opened a new and life-giving way through the curtain into the Most Holy Place* (10:19–20). Jesus echoes the same truth: *I am the way, the truth, and the life. No one can come to the Father except through me* (John 14:6).

All other means of approaching God are futile. God turns away from all other prayers because He looks only on what is holy. Believers are made this way through faith in Christ, who purifies us. Prayer only works for Christians—not unbelievers, atheists, agnostics, or even morally upstanding people. Prayers made by unbelievers are only acknowledged and answered when coupled with repentance and pleas for forgiveness.

Prayer is addressed to God, through Christ, and in the Spirit. *Now all of us can come to the Father through the same Holy Spirit because of what Christ has done for us* (Ephesians 2:18). God's Spirit leads us into His presence. The Spirit points out God, makes Him real, gives us access to Him, prays for us when we don't know how or what to pray for, and assures us we belong to God.

Believers can, and should, pray with confidence. God hears and is concerned with the details of our life and faithfully answers our sincere prayers. John says, *And we will receive from him whatever we ask because we obey him and do the things that please him* (1 John 3:22).

Verses 9 through 13 are usually referred to as the Lord's Prayer but are more appropriately named the Disciple's Prayer. The Lord's Prayer took place in the Garden of Gethsemane prior to His arrest. Additionally, Jesus would not ask for His sins to be forgiven.

Jesus spent an enormous amount of time in prayer and is our example of a healthy prayer life that accompanies real Christian living. Jesus rose early in the morning to pray and also sought moments of solitude at other times during the day. Prayer was the spiritual air He breathed. Prayer keeps our spiritual bodies functioning as air does our physical bodies. Prayer gave Jesus strength to fulfill His earthly ministry and should be a normal part of our existence. James reminds us, *The earnest prayer of a righteous person has great power and produces wonderful results* (5:16).

Jesus gives only a skeleton of prayer for the believer and doesn't expect us to limit our prayers to these exact words. They do, however, provide a good model.

Prayer recognizes God as our Father. Addressing Him in such a manner was a radical change and a challenge for those Jesus spoke to. During Old Testament times, a faithful Jew would never address God directly as Father. Jesus spoke primarily Aramaic, using the word *Abba*, which is comparable to the English word *daddy*. To the Jewish mind, addressing God in this fashion was improper and an act of irreverence to the highest degree. Faithful Jews knew God as their Father. He fathered the nation of Israel and set them apart as His special people. He was Savior to their nation, but over time, they lost this sense of intimacy.

Although God is not the Father of all people in the sense Jesus uses the term, He is Father to all in His position as Creator. Jesus, however, restricts God's Fatherhood relationship to believers.

Recognizing the fatherhood of God entails several encouraging elements that enhance our journey toward real living. We don't have to fear God in the sense of being afraid of Him. Our fear is holy reverence. We recognize Him as our creator and the sustainer and originator of our every breath. But we no longer fear judgment for our sins—Christ paid for them on the cross. We are no longer under condemnation. When love is perfected, it casts out fear: *Such love has no fear, because perfect love expels all fear. If we are afraid, it is for fear of punishment, and this shows that we have not fully experienced his perfect love* (1 John 4:18).

When God is our Father, uncertainties disappear and hope thrives. We are confident of God's love and concern for our life's details. Our hope is a confident assurance God has good plans in store for our future. Nor should loneliness overcome us. Jesus promised He would never leave or forsake His followers as they carry out His Kingdom work.

When God is Father, it settles selfishness. We understand our possessions come from God, are owned by him, and are given for our enjoyment and sharing with those in need—believers and unbelievers alike.

Our prayers should also include a desire for God to have preeminence in everything. We recognize the hallowness of His name. God desires and deserves priority in every area of our life. A person's name was important in Jewish thought. Names revealed something about their character and may have resulted from an episode. Isaac's name meant "he will laugh" because his mother laughed when told she would bear a son in her old age, and because Isaac brought joy to her (Genesis 21: 1-6).

God's name represents all He is, telling about His character, plan, and will. His name demonstrates faithfulness to what His name implies and is synonymous with His righteous character. The various names of God portray Him as creator, possessor of heaven and earth, provider, and lord of peace, but the clearest teaching about the Father came through Jesus Christ.

Hallowing God's name involves reverence, honor, and obedience. Our attitudes begin in the heart and then manifest themselves outwardly. We are aware of God's indwelling presence, which leads us to keep His temple—our body—clean from sinful practices and attitudes. We yearn for God's guidance in all of our life decisions and search for spiritual disciplines that will draw us into a more intimate relationship with him. Nor are we satisfied to enjoy this at the expense of others. We long to draw others into a similar experience.

When we pray for God's Kingdom to come, we recognize God has a program He wants us involved in, which is reflected in the Great Commission Jesus gave at the end of His earthly ministry: *Therefore, go and make disciples of all the nations, baptizing them in the name of the Father and the Son and the Holy Spirit. Teach these new disciples to obey all the commands I have given you. And be sure of this: I am with you always, even to the end of the age* (Matthew 28:19-20).

God's Kingdom has past, present, and future implications. The kingdom is past because God has always sovereignly ruled over individuals and history. It's present because God still rules. Jesus informed people His kingdom was in their midst. And it's future because Christ will return and rule solely as King of kings. God's kingdom is spiritual now, but later it will be literal.

We cannot pray for God's kingdom to come without being in it. Entering God's Kingdom happens by placing our faith in Christ's work on Calvary and connecting with Him in a trust relationship. When we're in, we want others in. Praying for the spiritual aspect of God's kingdom to come involves asking God to rule and reign in our lives.

Our ultimate aim is for God's will to be accomplished on earth as it is in heaven—bringing heaven to earth. This part of the prayer involves a paradox: God is sovereign, and yet we ask for His will to be done in our personal lives and to prevail over all the earth.

We may not know God's will in every situation, but some things are certain. God wants us to pray, study, and meditate on His Word. He wants us to fellowship and spread His love to the world. We also know He expects us to live pure, holy, and separated lifestyles. Additionally, God's will involves claiming His promises and working toward world peace.

Effective prayer acknowledges God's provision for our needs and demonstrates dependence on Him to meet these needs. This may seem out of place in industrialized countries where most people have enough stockpiled for weeks or even months. If they don't, they can readily visit a nearby grocery or retail store and purchase the needed staples. But hunger rages amidst the plenty. Homeless wander the same city streets as the affluent. Some countries are ravaged by famine and the starving must walk miles for a bowl of rice. Further, bread refers to more than daily food; it includes all our physical needs.

Although Creator and Controller and very busy, God concerns and obligates Himself to care for us. James verifies the same when he writes;

Whatever is good and perfect is a gift coming down to us from God our Father, who created all the lights in the heavens. He never changes or casts a shifting shadow (1:17).

Regardless of the self-efforts involved in attaining what we have, God is ultimately responsible. No matter how many talents or gifts we possess, we owe God for those, too. God prepared the Garden of Eden for humans before they were created, and He prepares our daily sustenance for us as well.

By asking God for daily bread, we affirm His supply in the past, acknowledge it in the present, and have faith it will be provided for the future. We make the request with confidence. While unbelievers receive the benefits of God's common grace—His sun shines and rain falls on them, too—He doesn't obligate Himself to supply their daily needs.

We also have the responsibility for meeting our daily needs. God normally supplies through our work efforts. According to Paul, if a person is able but chooses not to work, they shouldn't eat (2 Thessalonians 3:10). God obligates Himself, but we have accountability as well. God made the earth produce, but we have the responsibility of beginning and enhancing the process. Corn will grow, but only after the farmer plants it.

We petition God one day at a time, contenting ourselves with God's goodness and faithfulness of today and believing He will repeat it tomorrow and as long as we live. Nor does praying this relieve us of the responsibility to prepare for the future through savings and investments. As we pray for God to meet our daily needs, we should also ask Him to do the same for all people. Praying for others takes the focus from selfish concerns and expresses our love for all people.

Real-living prayers also recognize everyone needs God's forgiveness and that we should reciprocate the forgiveness God has given us. We owe a spiritual debt to God for our sins. It makes us susceptible to disease, illness, evil, and unhappiness—now and in eternity. The acts of sin witnessed daily through people's actions result from this common denominator.

Believers have a new nature but still struggle with the temptations of the flesh (old patterns of thinking and acting learned before coming to Christ). God forgives all our sins at salvation, but we still need His daily assurance they are forgiven. We need to confess daily, agreeing with God about our failures.

As God forgives, so should we. Sadly, we often find reasons not to. Forgiveness demonstrates our relationship with God and is the highest virtue we can possess. Unforgiveness leads to missing real living and demonstrates our failure to understand and appreciate God's forgiveness.

Believers also have the privilege of praying for God's protection from temptation and the assaults of our enemy. The root meaning of temptation involves testing or proving. God doesn't tempt—neither is He tempted—but He does allow Satan and his emissaries the freedom to tempt us.

When we really live, we avoid the danger and trouble sin creates. We desire to escape all prospects of falling into sin. While trials assist our spiritual, emotional, and mental growth, we must avoid putting ourselves in positions where the likelihood of sin increases. We should appeal to God to watch over our eyes, ears, mouth, feet, and hands.

Prayer is our right, privilege, and obligation. Through it we draw closer to our sovereign Creator, petition Him for our needs, intercede for others, express our confidence for strength through every trial, and thank Him for full and complete forgiveness. We live as He intends.

CHAPTER THIRTEEN

LEARN TO GIVE UP

MATTHEW 6:16–18

MAHATMA GANDHI IS FAMOUS FOR his fasts. He used them to get raises for Indian textile workers and also in his fight for India's independence from Britain. His were fasts unto death, and it is interesting how such an unimportant man could bring owners and governments to their knees when it appeared he would die.

Fasting is a practice that has been variously interpreted by believers and, at best, sporadically practiced. The Bible speaks of fasting on many occasions. While believers easily identify with the need to give and pray, fasting often seems like an unnecessary practice. Yet, those who choose to fast benefit spiritually and experience a level of real living that those who refuse to fast might miss out on.

By definition, fasting is abstaining from food or other things for a period of time to attain a spiritual result. Jesus fasted and probably assumed His followers would. But His instructions differed when He told people to fast and yet not look as if they were fasting. As He did with other misinterpretations of Scripture, Jesus corrected the meaning of fasting. Many of His contemporaries practiced it for bragging purposes only. They only wanted recognition.

While fasting isn't commanded, doing so does have spiritual and health benefits. We can fast from food in general, particular types of food, entertainment, types of communication, technology, sexual intimacy, or many other things.

During the Old Testament period, the Day of Atonement was the only occasion when fasting was commanded of the entire Israelite nation. Many fasted more frequently or at other times, but weren't required to. Fasting involved mourning and repenting of sin. From a one-day requirement, the practice spread to fasting when a national disaster was imminent or had occurred, and for other reasons.

The story of Jonah provides an example. God instructed him to go to Nineveh and preach against their wickedness. After preaching to city residents, the Bible says, *The people of Nineveh believed God's message, and from the greatest to the least, they declared a fast and put on burlap to show their sorrow* (3:5). A national disaster loomed on the horizon if they didn't alter their actions.

Another instance surrounds the death of King Saul and his son Jonathan. Saul was Israel's first king and fought their enemies, the Philistines. He and his sons met their death on Mount Gilboa. Men from Jabesh Gilead retrieved their bodies, and we read, *Then they took their bones and buried them beneath the tamarisk tree at Jabesh, and they fasted for seven days* (1 Samuel 31:13).

John the Baptist—Jesus' trailblazer—fasted, and his followers wondered why Jesus' disciples didn't fast. But fasting implies sorrow, and the disciples weren't sad. They had Jesus.

By the time of Jesus' arrival on earth, fasting had been perverted. Many religious leaders fasted on the second and fifth days, claiming these were the days Moses made his two trips to obtain the Ten Commandments. They also fasted on the major Jewish market days, because it gave them a larger audience. Old clothes, disheveled hair, makeup, dirt, and ashes accompanied the custom.

Fasting like this was a sham and mockery. They received praise from onlookers but not the more important person: God. Ceremonial fasting meant nothing to him, whether from food or anything else.

In the New Testament, the meaning of fasting changed. Early believers fasted, but not over personal sin. They set aside normal daily distractions to receive clear direction from God.

One example was when the gospel came to the Gentiles by way of Cornelius through Peter's ministry. Peter received a vision from God, instructing him to go to Cornelius' house. Cornelius was fasting when the word of God came to him, telling him to send for Peter.

The beginning of Paul's missionary journeys was connected to fasting. As the church at Antioch fasted, the Spirit instructed them to set apart Paul and Barnabas: *So after more fasting and prayer, the men laid their hands on them and sent them on their way* (Acts 13:3).

Fasting allows us to hear God more clearly and is appropriate when God directs us to it. Times of sorrow are appropriate times for fasting, as are periods of danger. Fasting may include confessing and mourning over sin and is always appropriate when beginning an important task or new venture. Whenever we fast—and for whatever reason—we should couple it with prayer and a sincere heart.

Christ gave His all for us, and we should be willing to abstain for Him so we are better equipped to serve Him and also to have a clearer vision of His future for us. Real living demands it.

CHAPTER FOURTEEN

OVERCOME WORRY

MATTHEW 6:19–34

BEING THING-ORIENTED IS NATURAL SINCE so much of our existence revolves around our play toys. We own them, or they do us, and perspective determines which. Vehicles take us to work and the kids to extracurricular activities. They transport us to church, doctors, dentists, optometrists, the grocery store, school, and afterschool activities. Homes protect us from the elements. Televisions, DVD's, Xboxes, cell phones, and computers keep us occupied at home, school, and work.

Possessions, in and of themselves, aren't wrong as long as we obtain them legally and keep a proper perspective. A wrong attitude about our possessions is what gets us into trouble. We want the newest version of play toys and go in debt to purchase them. Wrong perspective leads to coveting neighbors and peers' play toys or using the ones we have to commit crimes, destroy reputations, form addictions, or delve into immorality.

Needs such as food, shelter, and water are necessary for existence, but wants motivate us to make unnecessary purchases. The religious leaders of Jesus' time confused wants and needs and drew corrective teaching from Jesus. Jesus said it is impossible to serve God and mammon. Mammon refers to material possessions and comes from a root word meaning "to entrust" or "to place in someone's keeping." While originally meaning wealth entrusted to someone for safekeeping, it later came to mean "that in which someone trusts." We cannot serve two masters. We will hate one and love the other—or vice versa.

Nor is viewing wealth, health, and prestige as signs of God's approval correct. Job's experience disproves this theory. He was the most righteous person alive at the time but lost everything. God wanted to prove to Satan that Job's prosperity wasn't the reason Job served God. Job's wife and friends fell prey to prosperity theology. His friends told him he had hidden sin, and his wife suggested Job curse God and get it over with. Job maintained his integrity, and, in the end, God rewarded him with twice what he originally possessed. Job was never privy to the reason for his misfortunes, but God rebuked his friends for their misguided theology.

Earthly possessions are temporary. Jesus alludes to this when He tells what happens to them: moths eat them, rust destroys them, and thieves steal them. Knowing their temporary nature, it makes sense for us to store them in heaven rather than lay them up on earth. Laying up involves the idea of hoarding or stockpiling and presents a picture of unused wealth kept for the purpose of showing off or for creating an environment of laziness.

Jesus doesn't expect us to live in poverty. He didn't specifically require every one of His followers to give up everything. Both the Old and New Testaments recognize people's right to possess things, and God wants us to enjoy what He gives. Paul gives instruction that helps us walk the fine line: *Teach those who are rich in this world not to be proud and not to trust in their money, which is so unreliable. Their trust should be in God, who richly gives us all we need for our enjoyment* (1 Timothy 6:17).

Real living entails keeping our possessions—in whatever form they come in—in proper perspective. It means working hard, following ethical business principles, saving for our children when possible, and providing for our families. But we must also use our possessions in an outward way by giving to the needy and through supporting God's work.

How we use our possessions doesn't change their temporary nature. In ancient times, a person's wealth was often determined by the amount of clothing, grain, and livestock they owned, but these things were subject to destruction and theft. Even wealthy Solomon wrote, *In the blink of an eye wealth disappears, for it will sprout wings and fly away like an eagle* (Proverbs 23:5).

Job discovered the reality of Solomon's conclusion. He had a large family and vast amounts of livestock and servants, but his monument of possessions quickly crashed. One servant after another arrived with distressing news: the Sabeans stole his oxen and donkeys and killed his servants, fire from the sky burned up his sheep and even more of his servants, Chaldeans captured his camels and killed more servants, and wind destroyed the house where his children were partying—killing all of them.

Job responded by tearing his robe, shaving his head, falling to the ground, and crying: *I came naked from my mother's womb, and I will be naked when I leave. The LORD gave me what I had, and the LORD has taken it away* (Job 1:21).

Americans discovered the temporary nature of possessions when the stock market crashed in 1929, and a Great Depression followed. Economic failure led to more than 15 million people—one out of every four people—facing unemployment. People lost homes, farms, and money. Businesses faced enormous losses, and thousands of banks declared bankruptcy and closed.

Jesus says our focus should be on eternity where moth, rust, and thieves cannot penetrate. We only have time to focus on and serve one master—and God takes second seat to nothing and no one. Focusing solely on getting more signifies a malfunctioning spiritual heart. Christ is our Lord, not possessions, and giving our allegiance to anything or anyone else prevents us from experiencing real living.

These two masters—God and possessions—challenge us to do opposing things. One tells us to walk by faith while the other whispers for us to walk by sight. One proposes an attitude of humility while the other suggests pride will do. One advises us to keep our attention on things above while the other recommends we look below. One offers light; the other proposes darkness.

Our attitude about possessions reflects the health of our spiritual vision. Jesus says our eyes are the lamps of our bodies. When they are healthy, light fills our whole body, but if they are unhealthy, darkness will fill us.

The eye illustrates our heart, which in traditional biblical terms, is what controls and guides us and is synonymous with goals, dreams, and aspirations. Spiritually clear eyes are represented by single-minded devotion to God. Just as red eyes are painful and cause blurry vision, so do spiritually red eyes. They lead to distorted spiritual vision. Blurry spiritual eyes result when our lives are crowded with material concerns and are insensitive to spiritual things. Selfish indulgence in material things reflects poor spiritual vision.

When our perspective about our possessions is correct, generosity results. Jesus says a healthy eye leads to a body filled with light. Healthy entails the ideas of clear, simple, or single. Words closely related carry the idea of liberality. Living with our focus on others, along with a proper attitude about our possessions, leads to real living.

Our perspective on what we have determines in large part whether or how much we worry—something else that hinders real living. Worry comes from a German word meaning to choke or strangle, and it does this in all arenas of our life.

A reporter once asked a woman how she cared for her six biological children as well as the six she had adopted. The lady responded, "It's very simple. You see, I'm in a partnership." Seeing the reporter's confusion, the woman explained, "A partnership. One day a long time ago, I said to the Lord, 'Lord, I'll do the work if you do the worrying,' and I haven't had a worry since."

The list of things to worry about can be long and cumbersome. We can worry over how to maintain our possessions, how to get more stuff, how to make our money stretch to the next paycheck, and how to correct our wayward children. We can fret over being the victim of a crime, the prey of a terrorist act, or the target of a natural disaster. We can agonize over losing our investments, losing a child or spouse to death or disease, being placed in a nursing home, or having a spouse betray us.

All of us face situations that lead to worry—or at the very least anxiety—when we don't respond correctly to the situation. Jesus doesn't prohibit our concern over important matters, but rather our worrying about what He promises to supply: life's necessities. The wealthy are tempted to trust in money and material possessions while the poor are tempted to distrust God's provision when problems arise.

Concern over our earthly things is natural. After all, we live on earth and must have a limited amount of possessions to survive. But as believing earthlings, we should be more concerned with heavenly things.

Worrying demonstrates unfaithfulness toward God. Anxiety is not only dangerous but also foolish if God is our Master. The tense of Jesus' command not to worry entails stopping what we have already begun.

The life Jesus tells us to stop worrying about includes the physical, emotional, spiritual, and mental realms. Nothing justifies worry when Jesus is our Master, but it is probably the most committed sin we commit. Letting go and letting God is easier said than done.

Rather than worrying, Jesus wants us to learn contentment. Paul had mastered this—but it took him a lifetime. *Not that I was ever in need, for I have learned how to be content with whatever I have* (Philippians 4:11).

We attain this contentment when we remember God owns all things, controls all events, and provides for every need. God not only created all things, but also holds them together by His power. He will never take from us what belongs to Him. Nor do any events—seen or unseen—transpire without God initiating or permitting them. When Daniel was thrown into the lions' den for disobeying the king's command, it was not an anxious Daniel who lost sleep but the king (Daniel 6:18).

God provides everything we need. He can do so miraculously if need be, but more often He provides by giving us physical health and the ability to supply for ourselves. Even then, He is the provider. God demonstrated this ability to Abraham after asking him to sacrifice his promised son Isaac. As Abraham was about to slay the lad, an angel stopped him and showed him a ram in the thicket (Genesis 22:13).

God, however, doesn't obligate Himself to provide everything we might want—only those items necessary to sustain life: water, food, and clothing. Even these things pertain only to the body, and life entails more than meeting bodily needs. Life is not solely about adorning our bodies or spending enormous amounts of money trying to stave off the effects of aging. Our bodies live because God's breath sustains them, and our purpose is to glorify our Maker.

Jesus uses the birds to illustrate that worrying is unnecessary. Birds don't sow or reap, but get their life from God who gives them resources to gather and the instincts to do it. Birds are persistent in gathering but don't stockpile or worry about where their next meal will come from. If God cares for them, then surely He will provide for humans made in His image.

Jesus' second illustration concerns the longevity of life. Many are obsessed with this and demonstrate their passion through diets, physical exercise, and checkups—none of which are inherently wrong and, in fact, show wisdom. Foolish decisions can shorten our lives (worry included), and healthy practices may extend them. But nothing can force God to lengthen our lives beyond His designed end for us. We can worry ourselves to death, but not to life. Our primary concern should be obeying, pleasing, and glorifying God.

The third illustration relates to clothing. Jesus points to the lilies of the field and how God adorns them. Not even Solomon and his glorious kingdom could compare, but even flowers don't last forever. Dried grass and flowers were frequently used in ovens as fuel to bake bread. If God clothes the flowers, whose lifespan is very brief, He will do more for us.

Worrying about life's necessities calls into question God's love, integrity, and trustworthiness. Circumstances can't master believers who have mastered real living. When we worry, we are also being unreasonable. Worrying is inconsistent with our faith in God and makes our actions conflict with our words. If we're bound to worry, worrying about whether we are seeking the things of God and pursuing His kingdom and righteousness is wiser.

Worry is also unwise. Not only should we not worry about today, but we should also not worry about tomorrow. Jesus isn't forbidding preparation for the future. Not preparing is foolish and can put us and our family at risk.

Tomorrow will take care of itself because God controls it. Each day has enough trouble of its own, but even that trouble shouldn't concern us enough to result in worry. Real living leads us to concentrate our energies on meeting the trials, temptations, and tribulations of each day. God gives us strength and grace one day at a time—and will continue to do so until we take our final breath.

CHAPTER FIFTEEN

LOVE, DON'T JUDGE

MATTHEW 7:1–12

"DON'T JUDGE ME." A STATEMENT thrown around quite frequently in society. A statement designed to tell another person not to form an opinion about a person or their actions, and that many believe aligns with the Bible's teachings. However, a careful examination of what Jesus teaches here—along with other biblical teachings—will reveal that this is not at all what Jesus had in mind.

Psychologists identify a number of defense mechanisms we use for emotional protection. Projection is one and attributes to others undesirable characteristics the projector actually possesses. Examples are television evangelists caught in sins they adamantly rebuke in others or people criticizing others for gossiping, yet doing the same themselves. These and other examples just remind us that none of us are above falling into sin, so we should be careful what we say about others.

The type of judging Jesus references is hypocritical, unjust criticizing not a rebuke of forming opinions concerning right and wrong. Nor does it prohibit us from confronting wrong, which the Bible encourages in many places by specific command and example.

Judging unjustly is something we're all guilty of on occasion—probably more than we care to admit. We have a natural tendency to look for the bad in others, preferring to dig up dirt rather than cover it by helping them.

The media are experts at digging up dirt and prove it each time someone announces their candidacy for political office. We'd rather judge a homeless person's appearance than praise the beautiful whistle they have.

When we judge unfairly, we forget we also have dirt in our past. Everyone has skeletons in the closet. It's not our responsibility to resurrect them in other people's lives, lest Satan tempt us with the same thing we criticize others for. Paul warns of this, *Dear brothers and sisters, if another believer is overcome by some sin, you who are godly should gently and humbly help that person back onto the right path. And be careful not to fall into the same temptation yourself* (Galatians 6:1).

Jesus is not forbidding all criticism, evaluations, and judgments. I once knew a man who took such a narrow view. When I expressed my disagreement with him, he began a campaign to prove me wrong. His efforts degenerated into a nasty situation with him and his wife eventually leaving the church. Sometime later, he heard another preacher express my interpretation of Jesus' words, came to a different conclusion about his interpretation, and hunted me down to apologize.

So, what does Jesus teach? We have the responsibility to evaluate—and if necessary—make judgments about right and wrong. Failure to pronounce wrong as wrong leads to situational ethics—a prevalent philosophy. It teaches that whatever a person wants to believe or do is acceptable as long as it is to them. The Bible does not agree. We must judge between what is and is not sinful—but in a loving way that doesn't make us obnoxious to others. Had the church reformers of the sixteenth century avoided judgments about church life and its corruption, the Protestant Reformation would never have occurred.

Unfair and critical judging demonstrates an erroneous view of God. Jesus directed His criticism about unjust judgment toward the religious leaders. This parallels many of His other rebukes, which were also leveled against those belonging to the religious establishment, rather than those they considered desperately wicked.

A great many of the religious leaders' judgments were wrong and unrighteous. The reason for their profuse judgments was because they thought they were better than most people. They composed their own standard of religion and morality, twisting and adding to what God originally gave Moses. Many of their followers, in turn, replaced Scripture's authority with the traditions of the religious leaders—who tended to look down on those who didn't belong to their elite group. Their judgments were also often based on outward appearance and didn't take into account a person's heart—the thing they couldn't see.

A pertinent example is Jesus' story of the Pharisee and tax collector (Luke 18). Both men went to the temple to pray. Moving down front where all eyes could center on him, the Pharisee thanked God he wasn't a sinner like everyone else—especially the despised tax collector. He boasted of his service, fasting, and tithing. The tax collector, on the other hand, stood at the back and would not even lift his eyes to heaven. Rather, he acknowledged his sinfulness and cried out for God's mercy.

Preachers, prophets, teachers, and lay believers have always spoken out against sin. Doing so is a part of our duty. Neither does Jesus condemn the courts of law that are charged with binding or releasing those who've broken society's laws. Confronting sin is showing love because we know sin's consequences. To let others continue in their wicked ways without confronting them with God's truth and offer of forgiveness is a serious error and demonstrates disregard rather than love.

Yet, when we judge and criticize unjustly, we show an erroneous view of God who judges with mercy, righteousness, and equality. God judges according to His established standards of purity and holiness. Our judgment should parrot His, not the religious leaders. Nor should we judge by our standards and traditions when they don't align with God's. Condemning others leads us to play God, and we aren't the final court. Everyone will stand before God, not each other, for the final account.

Judging harshly and critically also demonstrates an erroneous view of others. Jesus warns against wrongly evaluating others simply because they don't measure up to our preconceived standards. This type of judging is carried out because we think we are superior and perfectly measure up to God's standards. But no one has ever accomplished this except Christ—and no one ever will.

Slipping into the kind of judgment Christ condemns proves easy. Examples are judging others for the kind of clothes they wear or the social class or race they belong to. Lists might also incorporate accents, peer groups, country or state of origin, and place of employment. Doling out cruel and unusual punishment through comments and criticisms is easier than searching for the good in others. Apart from Christ's forgiveness, we all stand as hopeless sinners. Race, social standing, ethnic background, and personal agendas are irrelevant. If not for God's grace, we would all be without hope.

Additionally, criticizing unjustly demonstrates an erroneous view of ourselves. Jesus warns against looking at the speck in other's eyes while missing the plank in our own. He also cautions against offering to remove the speck, while leaving the plank in ours. Attempting this makes us as guilty as the religious leaders of Jesus' day. Although we will never be sinless or without fault, we should attempt to clean up our known sins before trying to help someone else wash theirs. We must first take care of personal sins through disciplined spiritual practices that result in spiritual growth and discernment. Our responsibility is to carry each other's burdens, not add to them. Criticism is never appropriate until we have walked in the other person's shoes.

I recall a particular trip to the dentist to have cavities filled. He administered Novocain, waited a few minutes for it to take effect, and then started drilling. He quickly noticed the expression on my face, which said, "I can feel what you're doing." So, he waited a few more minutes before beginning again. When forced to judge, we should also show such love and concern—being quick to love but slow to criticize.

Understanding Jesus' teaching on judging enables us to better appreciate God's love and to align our actions with Jesus' teachings. After cautioning against unfair criticism, Jesus moves on to our relationships with other people and how love should characterize them. This is the positive side of His instruction. The absence of unjust judging doesn't necessarily mean we will love. Love involves action.

Loving others leads to success. Jesus says asking, seeking, and knocking will lead to results. This is a great and comprehensive promise. We are free to love and sacrifice for others because of Christ's love and His promise to meet our needs. When we don't have to worry about the depletion of our necessities, helping others takes on a different perspective.

Our Heavenly Father is a wonderful example. He expresses generosity in many ways. He sent Christ to pay for our sins. He blesses us presently and will throughout eternity, which frees us to serve others without fear of depleting our resources. We keep on asking, looking, and knocking, and, as we receive, we share.

But what are some things for which we should ask, seek, and knock? Wisdom and a closer walk with Christ should top the list. Wisdom helps discern and discriminate between right and wrong. James reminds us wisdom comes through prayer: *If you need wisdom, ask our generous God, and he will give it to you. He will not rebuke you for asking* (1:5).

God-given wisdom resulted in King Solomon's success. He was David's son and heir to the throne of Israel upon his father's death. He realized his awesome responsibility and petitioned God: *Give me an understanding heart so that I can govern your people well and know the difference between right and wrong. For who by himself is able to govern this great people of yours* (1 Kings 3:9)?

Wisdom is vital because of continuously changing situations. Technological advances present challenging ethical dilemmas. Imagine how many books, articles, or posts would be required for specific rules on every new and developing circumstance. We also need wisdom in our pursuit of a closer walk with God. His Spirit indwells us to encourage and strengthen us in our attempt.

Jesus' instruction to ask, seek, and knock, however, is not a blank check. The promise is made only to His followers. Obedience activates the promise: *And we will receive from him whatever we ask because we obey him and do the things that please him* (1 John 3:22). Our motives also enter the picture: *And even when you ask, you don't get it because your motives are all wrong—you want only what will give you pleasure* (James 4:3). And we must submit to God's will: *But when you ask him, be sure that your faith is in God alone. Do not waver, for a person with divided loyalty is as unsettled as a wave of the sea that is blown and tossed by the wind. Such people should not expect to receive anything from the Lord* (James 1:6–7). Additionally, perseverance is required, as seen in the tense of the verbs: keep on asking, seeking, and knocking.

Our requests are made known through prayer, which is active rather than passive. We do what we know God's will is while waiting for Him to unveil more. If praying for a job, we should look for one. If food is needed, we work. Real living entails trusting that God sees our needs more clearly than we do and is far ahead of us in fulfilling them.

Jesus' lesson is similar to not knowing what to buy a spouse, child, parent, or friend for Christmas. They seem to have everything. Because we're at a loss, we constantly tune in to any hints they drop. God knows our needs, but this doesn't relieve us from asking, knocking, and looking.

God's giving to us stimulates liberal giving to others. Paul writes, *Imitate God, therefore, in everything you do, because you are his dear children. Live a life filled with love, following the example of Christ. He loved us and offered himself as a sacrifice for us, a pleasing aroma to God* (Ephesians 5:1–2).

Jesus uses the illustration of a father's love. Loving fathers don't give children stones when they ask for bread. Nor do they give snakes when fish are requested or scorpions when eggs are demanded.

God gives liberally to His children and expects us to give identically. God isn't harsh, vengeful, or stingy. His treasure house has no limits, and no boundaries confine His goodness. If imperfect and human parents care for their children, how much more will a perfect heavenly father care for us.

God's love inspires equal treatment for everyone. Treating others as we want to be treated exemplifies the Golden Rule. The Golden Rule is a paraphrase of the second greatest command that requires us to love our neighbors as ourselves.

The Golden Rule teaching is found in the literature of almost every major religion and philosophy. The Jewish rabbi Hillel affirmed, "What is hateful to yourself, do not do to someone else." The Book of Tobit in the Apocrypha declared, "What thou thyself hatest, to no man do." Confucius alleged, "What you do not want done to yourself, do not do to others." And Epictetus, the Greek philosopher, said, "What you avoid suffering yourself, do not afflict on others."

Jesus' unique contribution comes in its positive reference, which makes our obedience more difficult. The verse becomes the straightedge by which we discern how morally crooked or off base our self-assessment and love toward others might be. Since God treats all equally, we should, too. He sent His Son to die for people of all races, cultures, and social classes. God's love extends to everyone, and ours must as well if we're to enjoy real living.

CHAPTER SIXTEEN

MAKE LIFE'S MOST IMPORTANT CHOICE

MATTHEW 7:13–14

BRITISH POET, JOHN OXENHAM, IN his poem, "The Ways," wrote:

> *To every man there openeth*
>
> *A Way, and Ways, and a Way,*
>
> *And the High Soul climbs the High Way,*
>
> *And the Low Soul gropes the Low,*
>
> *And in between, on the misty flats,*
>
> *The rest drift to and fro.*
>
> *But to every man there openeth*
>
> *A High Way and a Low*
>
> *And every man decideth*
>
> *The Way his soul shall go.*

Life is full of decisions. I remember a decision my daughter and I once had to make. We had planned an overnight backpacking trip, but the forecast called for severe thunderstorms. We chose to go anyway. We hadn't backpacked in nineteen years. She had aged . . . and so had I. We planned to set up camp after three miles and then pack a day bag and hike to a nearby mountain bald which boasted 360-degree views.

Making good time, we arrived at our campsite, set up our tent, hung our food, prepared a day bag, and set out for the bald. We could already hear thunder rolling across some of the nearby mountains. Climbing to the mountain summit involved a 1,000 foot elevation change and scaling many large rocks, but we made it. The view was spectacular . . . for about ten minutes. No sooner had we taken our pictures than dark clouds enclosed the mountains and their valleys. We, along with other sightseers, headed for cover.

On the way up, we had passed a gentleman coming from another direction. I asked him where his trail led to, and he said a parking lot. When we reached the intersecting trail on our way down from the summit, we headed for the parking lot, which had a stand-alone constructed porta-potty. We had no place to take shelter except the small overhang leading into the porta-potties.

The storm raged. Lightning streaked, thunder rolled, the wind howled, and hail fell. Other hikers headed for their cars. We had no such luxury. Eventually, we had to open the door to the porta-potty and stand inside. After forty-five minutes of enduring a tense situation in a smelly place, the storm moved on. A fellow hiker pointed us to the trailhead we sought, and we headed back to our tent.

Of the choices that face us, the decision to follow or not to follow Jesus is the most important. The Bible is replete with instances where God pleads with people to choose him.

While in the wilderness, God said through Moses to the nation of Israel, *Now listen! Today I am giving you a choice between life and death, between prosperity and disaster. For I command you this day to love the LORD your God and to keep his commands, decrees, and regulations by walking in his ways* (Deuteronomy 30:15–16).

After entering the Promised Land, Joshua challenged the Israelites to turn from the Egyptian and Canaanite gods to the Lord: *But if you refuse to serve the LORD, then choose today whom you will serve. Would you prefer the gods your ancestors served beyond the Euphrates? Or will it be the gods of the Amorites in whose land you now live? But as for me and my family, we will serve the LORD* (Joshua 24:15).

On Mt. Carmel, Elijah dared the people to choose between God and Baal: *How much longer will you waver, hobbling between two opinions? If the LORD is God, follow him! But if Baal is God, then follow him!* (1 Kings 18:21). In John's gospel, Jesus called on people to choose Him or another way, and we read, *At this point many of his disciples turned away and deserted him* (John 6:66).

Jesus invites His listeners to decide between His way and other ways. He has shared God's standards and told them what His kingdom is like. Now, His listeners were at the crossroads we all eventually approach, which involves a choice between divine and human righteousness.

Life's most important choice entails two gates: one narrow and the other wide. Entering is not an option, and trying to avoid one results in our automatically going through the other. Jesus wants everyone to enter the narrow gate leading to eternal life.

Jesus contrasts God's way of getting to Him with what many of the religious leaders were teaching the people (and what many still believe): that good works get us to God. Jesus said, *I am the way, the truth, and the life. No one can come to the Father except through me* (John 14:6), and, *Yes, I am the gate. Those who come in through me will be saved. They will come and go freely and will find good pastures* (John 10:9).

Entering the gate, Jesus says, is the way to God means coming a narrow way—not the way of the crowds. Such a narrow gospel often offends others because it requires that we repent of our sins. Jesus didn't preach salvation at any cost, nor did His disciples. Peter, appearing before the Jewish high court, said, *There is salvation in no one else! God has given no other name under heaven by which we must be saved* (Acts 4:12).

The other gate is wide and represents attempts to come to God by any way other than through Jesus. These endeavors represent efforts involving dependence on self or others but lead to a disappointing end. Many go this way, but security isn't found in numbers.

We must meet several requirements to enter the narrow gate. One, we must come alone. As the psalmist claimed the Lord was his shepherd (Psalm 23:1), so He must be ours. No one can come on our coattails, nor can we go on others'. We can only lead others to the narrow gate. Second, our approach to God must be devoid of any self-effort, other than expressing faith. God's grace is our only saving grace. We don't bring goodness or achievements but deny ourselves and yield everything to Jesus. Third, we must become like little children, depending solely on God's grace. A great exchange takes place as we trade what we are for what Christ offers. Finally, repentance is necessary and involves going in a different direction with our thoughts, actions, and attitudes.

In addition to two gates, life's most important choice involves two ways: one broad and the other narrow. The broad gate and the broad way parallel the narrow gate and the narrow way. Real living leads us to the narrow gate and down the narrow road. The psalmist says of those who come this way, *But they delight in the law of the LORD, meditating on it day and night. They are like trees planted along the riverbank, bearing fruit each season. Their leaves never wither, and they prosper in all they do* (Psalm 1:2–3).

The narrow way is difficult and demanding and involves self-denial. Conscious intense effort is required for us to walk this way. Doing so involves mourning over our sin while hungering for Christ's righteousness rather than our own.

Everyone not traveling the narrow road automatically walks the broad way. The broad way is easier and more attractive. It's the way of least resistance where we can be in the center. It's also easier, like floating downstream. Many trek this way, but there is no security in numbers. The writer of Proverbs shares, *There is a path before each person that seems right, but it ends in death* (14:12).

The gates and paths have two destinations and are traveled by two groups. Both point to the good life, but only one actually delivers. Following the narrow way of Christ leads us to real living and abundant life. The broad way is heavier populated, allows us to do what we want, and paints a picture of the good life—but has a disappointing end.

CHAPTER SEVENTEEN

LISTEN TO THE WARNINGS

MATTHEW 7:15–20

"IF YOU PLAN TO PLACE poison on a shelf where you have healing medicines, label it clearly." A pertinent warning—only one of which fill our lives.

Cigarette packs warn of lung cancer and other medical problems. Medicines caution against taking them if you have high blood pressure, heart trouble, prostate trouble, or stomach trouble. Taking certain other medications with them, or giving them to underage children, can also be dangerous. And of course, warning signs litter the highways, interstates, and roads: signs that caution against railroad crossings, ice on bridges, sharp curves, and steep inclines.

President Wilson repeatedly warned Germany before he involved the United States of America in World War I. He warned them first after they sank the British passenger liner Lusitania, which carried several American passengers, then again after the Sussex went down killing more Americans. Germany ignored the warnings and continued to sink ships carrying American passengers. President Wilson finally petitioned Congress for a Declaration of War.

Jesus now warns against those who would try to deceive us. False prophets were not new to the Jewish people. Moses had warned, *Suppose there are prophets among you or those who dream dreams about the future, and they promise you signs or miracles, and the predicted signs or miracles occur. If they then say, "Come, let us worship other gods"—gods you have not known before—do not listen to them* (Deuteronomy 13:1-3).

Jesus did the same: *Don't let anyone mislead you, for many will come in my name, claiming, "I am the Messiah." They will deceive many* (Matthew 24:4-5). And so did John: *Dear friends, do not believe everyone who claims to speak by the Spirit. You must test them to see if the spirit they have comes from God. For there are many false prophets in the world* (1 John 4:1). When Paul met with the Ephesian elders on the beach near Miletus, he said to them, *I know that false teachers, like vicious wolves, will come in among you after I leave, not sparing the flock* (Acts 20:29).

False teachers usually gain a hearing and a following. People look for someone or something to believe in. Why else would thousands have followed Adolf Hitler and committed the crimes he asked them to? Jesus warned because He knew we needed to be alert for those who would try to deceive us.

False prophets are dangerous because they normally claim to speak for God or a higher power. Tragically, they are often welcomed. In speaking to Jeremiah, God said, *The prophets give false prophecies, and the priests rule with an iron hand. Worse yet, my people like it that way* (5:31).

False prophets are more dangerous than those who claim no affiliation with God because they are often on the inside. They destroy us instead of caring for and nurturing us. Even well-meaning believers can unknowingly allow Satan and his forces to use them to wreak havoc in God's churches by causing division and creating conflict.

The religious leaders of Jesus' day were prime examples of false prophets. They pretended to care for God's people and to have their best interests at heart. They faked interest in their souls and claimed to represent them before God. Yet they had their own interests at heart and were looking out for themselves.

Jesus tells us to guard against such people. They are like beasts preying on the weak and unsuspecting. Wolves were the enemy of Palestinian sheep, searching for strays and stragglers. False prophets are clever and wily like wolves. Guarding against them requires placing ourselves on high spiritual alert.

False prophets come in sheep's clothing. People normally recognized prophets of old by what they wore. Elijah donned rough and uncomfortable clothing. John the Baptist dressed in a coat of camel's hair. Shepherds wore clothing made of wool. By impersonating a genuine shepherd, a false shepherd could deceive the sheep.

The People's Temple Christian Church led by Jim Jones was a horrifying example of where following a false prophet can lead. Many of his disciples had been reared in Christian homes. Some saw a chance for higher Christian fellowship and service. Jones knew how to inspire hope. He seemed to care for them and performed many needed services. He preached, claimed to cast out demons, and performed miracles and healings. He created what appeared to be a warm Christian community, but warning signs abounded for the perceptive. In the end, almost one thousand of his followers committed suicide in the jungles of Guyana, South America, thinking they were serving God.

David Koresh, leader of the Branch Davidians in Waco, Texas, was another example. At times, he claimed to be God's Son. By the time his fiasco ended, he had led his followers to a burning inferno.

Looking out for false prophets involves self-examination. Our spiritual fruit lets us know who we and others are—just as glancing at a fruit tree reveals its species. God's followers are characterized by at least two things: we are commissioned by God, and we carry His message. Paul lists the fruit we should bear: *But the Holy Spirit produces this kind of fruit in our lives: love, joy, peace, patience, kindness, goodness, faithfulness, gentleness, and self-control* (Galatians 5:22–23).

Jesus illustrates His point by appealing to a grapevine and a fig tree. Grapes are not gathered from thorn bushes, nor are figs collected from thistles. From a distance, they may appear to be a fig tree or a grapevine, but closer investigation reveals their true nature.

A close examination of our motives, standards, attitudes, and works shows others where our loyalties lie. Though not saved by good works, we are saved to generate them. In addition to producing the fruits of the Spirit, our deepest desire should be glorifying and honoring God. This is real living.

Jesus concludes this section by mixing in a warning about the coming judgment. As trees not bearing fruit are cut down and used for cooking and heating, so people not bearing fruit will one day experience eternal punishment. This is the destiny of false prophets and all who reject God . . . the end for all who enter the broad gate and walk the broad way. God doesn't destroy them; they destroy themselves by coming the wrong way and producing the wrong fruit.

CHAPTER EIGHTEEN

KNOW YOUR IDENTITY

MATTHEW 7:21–27

HAVING TAUGHT MIDDLE SCHOOLERS, I have witnessed hundreds of efforts to determine identity. Suddenly at ten or eleven years of age, young boys and girls don't know who they are anymore. They may question long-held beliefs and traditions held by their families. They often speak hateful words to their parents and vow not to be like them when they grow up. A simple question from a parent can set off a volcanic eruption. Psychologists term this magnification—blowing things out of proportion. Through interacting with their peers—some good and some not so good—middle schoolers form their own identity, one they may or may not change later on. Associating with the wrong peers can lead them to false conclusions about their identity.

Being deluded about our spiritual identity can also occur—thinking we're okay with God and are on our way to heaven when we might not be. Some imagine attending church or making sure we do more good than bad works is enough. Others take confidence in being born into a Christian nation or home. Still others suppose God will simply overlook our sins and let us enter heaven because of our association with someone or because of our family history.

At one church I attended, an older gentleman stood and gave his testimony. Sadly, it had nothing to do with repentance or faith, but how at a certain age, he had walked a church aisle and joined the church. Many people associate church membership with salvation. Jesus spoke to listeners who were thought a mere verbal profession of association with God was enough or who assumed intellectual knowledge about God was sufficient.

The Bible details high standards by which to judge an authentic Christian lifestyle. It also warns against self-deception. Several things can lead us into spiritual self-deception. Some look to walking a church aisle, taking a preacher's hand, asking to join a church, saying a prayer, undergoing baptism, or performing some other ritual. Others fail to examine themselves by looking at their inner motives, standards, and desires to see if they honor God. Paul instructs, *Examine yourselves to see if your faith is genuine. Test yourselves* (2 Corinthians 13:5).

Authentic religious activities can be associated with such undertakings as attending church, reading the Bible, praying, or performing other religious rituals. But these efforts should not be viewed with the idea fair exchange—that our life's good and bad will balance out with the good outweighing the bad.

Thinking we have experienced real Christian living just because we said some words or prayer is dangerous. Jesus said not everyone who calls Him Lord will enter heaven, but only those who do the will of His Father.

The term Lord showed honor and respect. As used here, it probably substituted for Yahweh—the name for God that was too holy to speak. That these hypothetical individuals had done so many things in Jesus' name implies they did more than respect Him. Jesus referenced those who had made a profession to follow Him and had followed it up with good works.

But based on what Jesus says, not everyone who calls on Him in life will be acknowledged by Him after death. The rejected are those who chose the wide gate and walked the broad way. Their works are impressive, but their lives don't bear out what their lips profess. We can only conclude that a verbal profession does not necessarily equate with faith.

I've heard similar statements. Testimonies by those who prayed a prayer at a young age but later realized they weren't sincere or didn't understand what they had done. Or by those who made verbal professions but later left the church, never to return. A pattern of life-long obedience is the clincher for real living. A faith relationship with Christ demands this. Salvation and obedience go hand in hand. Those whom Christ claims not to know haven't lost or forfeited their salvation; they never had it.

Martin Luther, leader of the Protestant Reformation, is a noteworthy example of the people Jesus refers to. He left a secular occupation to enter a monastery of Augustinian monks. He made progress, was ordained as a priest, studied Scripture faithfully, and obtained a doctorate of theology. Had you asked him if he believed in Christ, he would have said most definitely. He would also have testified he believed in the death and resurrection of Christ. Yet, he did not know about being born again—what Jesus told Nicodemus was necessary—and it wasn't until Luther understood this that he became the great church reformer.

Nor does intellectual knowledge necessarily equal real Christianity. The ones who hear but don't do represent those who think it does. Those who hear and do are similar to the wise man who built his house on a foundation with underlying rock. Those who hear and don't do are like the foolish man who built his house on sand. The wise man's house survived the storm, but the foolish man's experienced destruction. The solid foundation is our faith in Jesus Christ.

Both builders had similarities and differences. Both heard the gospel and the way of salvation. Each had built a house that represented their life. The wise man's house was secure because his house was built on God's Word. The foolish man thought his was because he had heard the Word of God, was born in a Christian nation, was raised in a Christian home, etc. Both believed their houses would stand, but one based his confidence on God, while the other depended on himself or others. The difference was the foundation.

Intellectual knowledge falls short of a real relationship with Christ. We must hear, believe, and do. The Bible commands us to do the Word of God, not just hear it (James 1:22). Building on the rock is difficult and involves self-emptying. Life on the sand is the opposite. This life is easily accomplished because it's constructed on selfishness. Life on the rock is real and will stand the storm of God's judgment and the trials of life, but religious rituals and intellectual knowledge without faith puts us on a sand foundation that is destined for destruction.

CONCLUSION

REAL LIVING MAY INVOLVE RULES, regulations, and traditions, but they do not produce it. Believing that it does results in building our life house on sand, and, in the end, it won't stand. We experience real living by incorporating Jesus' two greatest commands into our lives: love Him supremely and then others as ourselves. The first will always result in the second, and when we obey these two commands, we will fulfill all the other demands of God's moral law. Abundant life will be ours. We'll learn to be content no matter our circumstances, we'll allow Christ to accomplish His plan through us, and we'll store our true treasures in heaven where we plan to live eternally.

ABOUT THE AUTHOR

MARTIN WILES IS AN AUTHOR, English teacher, minister, and freelance editor currently residing in Greenwood, South Carolina. He is the founder and editor of Love Lines from God (*www.lovelinesfromgod.com*). Wiles is the Managing Editor for *Christian Devotions*, the Senior Editor for *Inspire a Fire*, and a Proof Editor for *Courier Publishing*. He has also served as Web Content Editor for Lighthouse Publishing of the Carolina. Wiles has authored *A Whisper in the Woods: Quiet Escapes in a Noisy World* (Ambassador International), *Grits & Grace & God* and *Grits, Gumbo, and Going to Church* (Lighthouse Publishing of the Carolinas), *Morning By Morning, Morning Serenity*, and *Grace Greater Than Sin* (America Star Books) and is a contributing author in *Penned from the Heart* (Son-Rise Publications), and *Rise* (Chaplain Publishing). He has served as Regional Correspondent and Sunday school lesson writer for the *Baptist Courier* and has also written for Lifeway's Bible Studies for Life curriculum. He has also been published in *Christian Living in the Mature Years, Mature Living, Open Windows, Proclaim, The Secret Place, The Word in Season, Upper Room, Light from the Word, Reach Out Columbia, Mustard Seed Ministries, Journey Christian Newspaper, Common Ground Herald, The Quiet Hour, Power for Living, Halo Magazine, Joyful Living Magazine, Christian Broadcasting Network, Sharing, Today's Christian Living, These Days, Plum Tree Tavern, Eskimo Pie, The Scarlet Leaf Review, Creation Illustrated, LIVE, Purpose Magazine, Stand Firm, The Banner*, and *Lutheran Digest*. He is a regular contributor to *Christian Devotions, PCC Daily Devotions, Theology Mix, Inspire a Fire*, and is a regular columnist for the Dorchester County *Eagle Record*, the Orangeburg County *Times and Democrat,* and the Greenwood County *Index Journal.*

SMALL GROUP STUDY GUIDE

CHAPTER ONE

1. What are some of the dos and don'ts you grew up with? How did they color your perception of God?

2. What are some ways people search for meaning in life?

3. What are some proper ways we can mourn over sin and over losses in life?

4. How have you experienced gentleness? How have you given it?

CHAPTER TWO

1. How important is it that our inward beliefs express themselves in outward actions?

2. What are some ways we can show mercy to others?

3. In what ways can we cultivate a pure heart?

4. What are some ways we can promote peace in our world?

5. What types of persecution have you faced because of your stand for Christ?

CHAPTER THREE

1. Why is influence important?

2. Name some ways others have positively influenced you.

3. Why is integrity important to our influence?

CHAPTER FOUR

1. What are some opinions you have heard about God's Word?
2. Why does it matter what we think about the Bible?
3. What impact should the Bible have on our lives?

CHAPTER FIVE

1. Discuss whether you think anyone or anything can make you angry?
2. What are some ways we can process anger without it leading to sin?
3. Shares some situations where you got angry. Then, tell how you could have better handled them.

CHAPTER SIX

1. Share some ideas you have heard from others about sexual relationships outside of marriage or prior to marriage.
2. Think of some ways you can prepare ahead of time to deal with sexual temptation.
3. What are some practical ways we can take Jesus' teaching on sexual faithfulness to our society?

CHAPTER SEVEN

1. Define what you think marriage means.
2. What are some necessities for a successful marriage?
3. Share some things that have made your marriage better.
4. How can the church help those who are struggling in their marriages or who have experienced failed marriages?

CHAPTER EIGHT

1. Why is keeping our word important?
2. Discuss the importance of absolute truth.
3. What are some consequences of people not keeping their word?

CHAPTER NINE

1. Discuss each of the rights Jesus says we should be willing to give up?
2. Give reasons why it is difficult to give up these rights.
3. Share some instances where you gave up one or more of these rights. How did it make you feel?

CHAPTER TEN

1. Discuss Jesus' teaching about loving our enemies.
2. How had God's command to love others been corrupted by Jesus' time?
3. What are some reasons we have trouble loving those who don't love us?
4. What are some practical ways we can show love for our enemies?

CHAPTER ELEVEN

1. What are some reasons we might find it difficult to give with the proper motives?
2. What are some practical ways we can show our love for God and others through our giving?
3. Name some steps we can take to prevent our giving for the wrong reasons.

CHAPTER TWELVE

1. Discuss some things that confuse you about prayer.
2. What are some things that make forgiveness difficult, and how can prayer make it easier?
3. Share some prayer habits that have drawn you closer to God?
4. Discuss each element of the "Lord's Prayer."

CHAPTER THIRTEEN

1. Discuss some reasons people fast.
2. Discuss some of the benefits of fasting.
3. What are some inappropriate reasons to fast?

CHAPTER FOURTEEN

1. What are some signs that we don't see our possessions with the correct perspective?
2. Why do we think we need more and more play toys?
3. What are some steps we can take to stave off worry?
4. What does worry say about our relationship with God?

CHAPTER FIFTEEN

1. Discuss what Jesus really taught about judging.
2. What are some ways we can confront this misinterpreted teaching of Jesus when we hear it in society?
3. What are some practical steps we can take to confront prejudice in all of its forms?
4. Name some ways we can demonstrate the Golden Rule in our lives.

CHAPTER SIXTEEN

1. Discuss what Jesus taught about the narrow and wide gates and about the narrow and broad roads.

2. Share ways we can lead others to the narrow gate and narrow path without being offensive.

3. What are some ways we can defend what Jesus says about how people must come to Him?

CHAPTER SEVENTEEN

1. Share a time when you met a false teacher?

2. What are some ways we can guard against succumbing to false teachers?

3. Why do people seems to easily fall to false teachings?

CHAPTER EIGHTEEN

1. What are some things we base our identity on?

2. According to Jesus, how can we know without a doubt that He will accept us?

3. What are sand foundations we might build our lives on that won't last?

A
WHISPER
IN THE
WOODS

QUIET ESCAPES
IN A NOISY WORLD

MARTIN WILES

A WHISPER IN THE WOODS: Quiet Escapes in a Noisy World was birthed from Martin Wiles' numerous treks with his two children and his middle brother in mountainous areas on the eastern coast of the United States. Through these hiking and camping experiences, God taught him valuable lessons that have seen him through many difficult life experiences.

Martin's weekly devotionals found in *A Whisper in the Woods* take the reader out of the noise that often accompanies living in this world and into the quiet escapades of wooded areas where the voice of God is more clearly heard.

As you walk with Martin through the mountain valleys and over the high summits, you too will hear God whisper words of comfort to you.

For more information about
Martin Wiles
and
Don't Just Live . . . Really Live
please visit:

www.lovelinesfromgod.com
www.facebook.com/martinwilesgreenwoodsc
www.twitter.com/linesfromgod
www.instagram.com/lovelinesfromgod
www.linkedin.com/in/martin-wiles-5a55b14a

For more information about
AMBASSADOR INTERNATIONAL
please visit:

www.ambassador-international.com
@AmbassadorIntl
www.facebook.com/AmbassadorIntl

If you enjoyed this book, please consider leaving us a review on
Amazon, Goodreads, or our website.

More Inspirational Nonfiction from Ambassador International

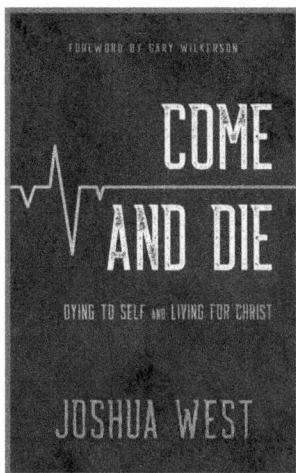

In *Come and Die*, Pastor Joshua West explores the Scriptures and extrapolates verses to show just what Christ means when He tells his followers to "take up your cross and follow Me." Are you brave enough to accept His call, or will you continue to live this shallow, empty life that holds no eternal meaning or reward?

Whether we realize it or not, we all have an internal belief system—a worldview—which directs our thoughts and actions and shapes how we understand the world around us—where we came from, how we should live, and what our purpose is. Examining your personal worldview in light of God's Master Story can strengthen your faith and clarify your purpose in this world.

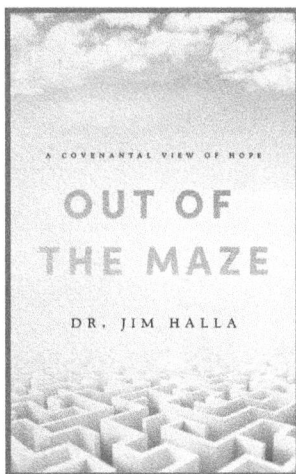

In *Out of the Maze*, Jim Halla gives a fresh look at hope, by implementing it God's way. He shows the difference between true hope and false hope, on hope in self and hope in God. This book provides a self-inventory to discover true hope and that hope doesn't depend on circumstances or people.

www.ingramcontent.com/pod-product-compliance
Lightning Source LLC
Chambersburg PA
CBHW070906100426
42737CB00047B/2885